tip of the iceberg

larry o'connor

tip of the iceberg

the university of georgia press

athens and london

Published by the University of Georgia Press
Athens, Georgia 30602
© 2002 by Larry O'Connor
All rights reserved
Designed by Betty Palmer McDaniel
Set in 12/16.5 Centaur by Bookcomp, Inc.
Printed and bound by Maple-Vail
The paper in this book meets the guidelines
for permanence and durability of the Committee
on Production Guidelines for Book Longevity
of the Council on Library Resources.

Printed in the United States of America
02 03 04 05 06 C 5 4 3 2 1

Library of Congress Cataloging-in-Publication Data

O'Connor, Larry, 1955–
    Tip of the iceberg / Larry O'Connor.
        p. cm.
    ISBN 0-8203-2356-X (alk. paper)
    1. O'Connor, Larry, 1955– 2. Fathers and sons—Canada.
    3. Canada—Biography. I. Title.
    CT310.O36 A3 2002
    971.064'092—dc21   2001043069

British Library Cataloging-in-Publication Data available

to mary

The real Canadian is a northerner.

ROBERTSON DAVIES

I was alone on the ice.

JANET FRAME

contents

of the library at grade school. I had moved it from History to Insect and Garden, where people seldom came by, and I looked at it every chance I could get. I didn't ponder lost treasures on the sea floor, families who would never see their loved ones again, the pointlessness of the loss. I could not have cared less for the dead. The only gold I had ever seen was plated on Father's watch; the only silver, the coins Mum kept in a cigar box on her bedroom dresser. None of my relations—poor farmers in Canada, footsoldiers in England—were scarcely able to sail aboard elegant ocean liners. None, as far as I knew, had even learned to swim.

Instead, I was drawn to the floating mountain of ice. Ten times the size of the *Titanic*, the iceberg loomed beneath the ocean surface, its dark mass going off the page. The tip of the iceberg shuddered with the weight of what lay beneath.

Most winters we had a skating rink out back. From the time I was nine years old, I watched my father flood the rink. Night after winter night, Father stood outside in the cold while I rested my head against crossed arms on the kitchen table and watched him through the window. Behind me, from another room, the television shone like a blue moon. Before me, my father, a shadowy figure in a dark coat, his fedora tugged down his forehead like a laborer in a Van Gogh, watered the rink.

Except for a gentle tossing motion of his right wrist, Father was still. Mist rose from the long snake of a hose and from the spots where water fell. Water that didn't freeze on contact flowed in rivulets, covering the rink, filling the low spots.

I was waiting for a wink, a sidelong glance, a doff of the fedora, anything. But it didn't happen. He didn't once look up from the ice.

Father was a loner who in all seasons worked underground at his basement workshop. I was his nervous child, who for the first twelve years of life barely spoke. When I was two my sister, Helen, obliged my desire for chewable cherry-flavored aspirins by feeding me twenty-four of them, one after the other. No more, she said, turning over the empty bottle. To her credit, Helen told Mum and I was rushed to the hospital, where the family doctor told my parents that it didn't look like I would make it. I pulled through—like a hand-me-down from a wringer washer—and grew up thin and sickly, a stripling who put on six pounds a year. In ninth grade I was four-foot-eight and eighty-nine pounds. "Put some meat on your bones, boy," Father said, as Mum whispered behind his back. Be easy on him. He's a miracle, after all, a boy who was gone and then was not. Rushed to Keppel General a lump of clay and sent back delicate china. Touched by God, eh?

Most days in winter Father left to go to work before I got up in the morning and arrived home late at night. Then he wolfed down the meal Mum left warming on the stove and went to flood the rink. I wondered if he were a phantom like the projectionist at the Roxy whose identity was a town mystery. I believed my father was more than just a traveling salesman, more than an icemaker, but what I didn't know.

Others on my block had fathers whom I never got a strong sense of; they were like spirits who only came out at night. Beginning at dusk, the boys and girls of the block turned to look at every set of

Like a poem the north walked in my mind as I watched, knowing that Nanook of the North and his family died of cold and starvation a year after the film was shot.

My mother came to know my father when he was a repairman and driver for Mickey's Electric. They met at a dance in the pavilion on the outskirts of Keppel's town park, and then my father drove my mother down tree-lined lanes in a black truck with a picture of Mickey Mouse painted on its side. Father had two other jobs then—floor salesman at a lumber yard and telephone solicitor for a department store—but Mum said his job as electrician for Mickey was "Numero Uno." Father liked being his own boss in job after job, house after house. He liked to pull and sort colored wire, cover them up, and screw the plates down tight.

That first year they drove to dances at the park, and then Father took Mum home, to where she lived with her parents. Father replied in monosyllables, saying "Sure" and "Yup" as Mum talked in sing-song melodies about her day at the Bell as a telephone operator. Grandfather urged Mum to find out more about Father and his family or stay clear. But Grandfather would only go so far, and he never interviewed Father about his intentions. "She's twenty-one," he said. "You have to hope for the best."

Mum chose not to see anything sinister in my father's silences. The youngest of a working-class family of nine, Mum was no child of intimacy. Once as they were strolling Sauble Beach, a shoreline of fix-'em-up clapboard cottages, Father plucked a blue pebble from the sand and placed it in her hand. "We'll live here one day," he said, "just you and me." Mum nodded, touched by the insistence in his glare. She would keep the pebble and one day display it atop the mantle in the beach place my father would build.

After about a year of dancing cheek to cheek and driving around Keppel, exchanging furtive glances from the vinyl bucket seats of Mickey's truck, Mother and Father were married.

Northern explorers lived extraordinary lives, but they've been forgotten all the same. Take Hudson Stuck, for instance. A century ago, Hudson Stuck froze his Adam's apple. Billy Hardy, a boy I remember from childhood, once froze his tongue to a bicycle rack during a cold snap and wasn't freed until an acetylene torch warmed a section of the bars. Of the frozen Adam's apple, Stuck said, "It was a most inconvenient thing to freeze." Billy Hardy's screams were muffled for a month.

Hudson Stuck survived the "strong cold," a land where water was like iron and stillness and silence reigned. In the strong cold, a bare hand less than a minute in the open turns bone white. Stuck traveled along riverbeds—the only route free of obstructions in dense northern forests—but by doing so endured temperatures that were twenty to thirty degrees more frigid than that of the bush. Body heat seemed "feeble and futile to contend with its crushing power. The cold holds all living things in its relentless grip."

Victorian explorers weren't much for showing signs of weakness or fear. "It seems a pity, but I do not think I can write more" was the last line written in the official diary of Robert Falcon Scott, the doomed English explorer. Then he froze to death. Two weeks before, Titus Oates, the weakest and most feverish of the company, had struggled to his feet inside a bitterly cold tent and told his comrades,

"I am going outside and may be some time." He intended to walk to his death (and needed to piss), but for matters of pride and propriety withheld these intentions—an ability to go long periods of time without relieving themselves was a point of pride among Victorians. The next day Oates was found frozen solid. Weeks later every member of Scott's expedition was dead. Their bodies, encased in ice for one hundred years, will soon calve into the sea.

Grandfather was a Victorian by nature. As a young man he had volunteered in the British Army to fight in the First World War, and until his old age he walked erect, unflinching, his head full of marching music. He never traveled to the far north, but he was fascinated with the idea of the place and told me stories of English explorers and Eskimo myth. Like thousands of others in his generation, Grandfather not only chose to leave England behind after the War, but friends and family there, too. Attachments beyond a taste for porridge, an ear for "Tipperary," were feckless, unworthy. Grandfather wasn't one to get personal, but he had a way of drawing attention to himself with simple gestures. Like at an intersection when the light would change: He would never anticipate the change from red to green, never step off the curb a second too soon. No one entered the street with more authority, more righteous claim to the pavement under his feet than my mother's father.

When I think of the tragedy of Scott, a man in Navy-issue woolens dying by inches from the cold, I see my grandfather's stony face, his unblinking eye.

My sister was born first. Father was consolidating new territory in his traveling salesman's job when Mum had to go to the hospital. The day Helen was born my father was driving samples of Hula Hoops and bubble blowers to new accounts, offering them introductory specials. A great fad was coming, he had said. He told them to buy. I was born a year later, when my father was Numero Uno, this time as salesman of candy bars and toasters for the Hudson's Bay Company. He was on the road a lot then and wasn't home for a week after I was born. Iris, my aunt, whose husband, Bill, worked in a factory that made fancy-glass Christmas ornaments, and their girls Debbie, Donna, and Dell all held me before my father did.

Father was always out of the house, finding ways to bring home more money. For years he worked instead of taking his two-week annual vacation, picking up the slack for salesmen who took theirs. Once, he mortgaged heavily to buy a dilapidated apartment building, which kept him busy as superintendent with wiring and carpentry chores. I was five, maybe six, so small for my age, and quiet, I think at times Mum and Father forgot that I was there. Like the time Father was working on the front verandah on a stepladder, fixing an outdoor light. An attractive brunette walked by on the sidewalk, and he turned and wolf-whistled so loudly and with such relish that I found I couldn't withhold the retelling of the remarkable effect to Mum, who listened with the keenest of interest and then went out to put on a performance of her own.

Otherwise, Father was sullen, gray. Like a stranger who had followed us home from the supermarket. When he wasn't driving the green company car loaded with samples, he was shoveling snow from the walk or hammering something at the basement worktable. In winter he woke at dawn, worked ten hours a day, came home in darkness, and flooded the rink. In summer he was busier. Some Sundays he would drive us to Sauble, where one of mother's brothers, Stan, rented a cottage. But mostly he worked because, he said, tourist season was good for business.

It was after my brother, Jim, was born that Mum made the stand of her life. Father was away from home on a course at Kodak in Rochester, New York, that he needed to take in order to sell thirty-five-millimeter cameras and the new Instamatics. Mum told him the minute he got home that he would have to arrange for a week off around the birth of the next baby. Father looked at her as if she'd gone mad. "What's next? Disposable diapers?" he said. She got the diapers, not the child.

Mum's mother died early. Of cancer. A pale woman with razor-thin lips and perfect posture, Frances Bloodworth was sick at Mum's wedding. She was immaculate in a gray suit and black felt hat, smiling serenely, presiding as the guest of honor, the mother of the bride, this ninth child she barely knew. How much could she have known of the children raised on a carpenter's salary in a foreign town, a place of buried bottles, a forwarding post for doomed explorers? Bow and curtsy, boys and girls. Shut your mouth when you chew.

Frances Bloodworth did what was expected. She presided over weddings, even for this last girl, a sweet, quiet unassuming one, who wasn't sure of what she was doing, wondering perhaps if she were making a mistake. But Frances Bloodworth did not interfere. She had done what she could—for all of them—nine children married into Canadian-born families, local folks. Sure to have children of their own, and if God was good, to follow in Frances Bloodworth's footsteps and preside over the weddings of their own children, chock full of cancer and not showing the pain. To sit for the wedding photo, straight-backed and proud, never wincing—not once—because there is no greater legacy for the English poor than to sacrifice with munificent grace.

The English went north gloriously unprepared. A friend of Franklin's, Sir William Edward Parry, first wintered his ship and crew in the north almost two hundred years ago. Men who left their skin unprotected in the strong cold had layers of flesh ripped off when it brushed metal. Lemon juice and vinegar froze solid, breaking containers. Piss turned red; beards bleached white. If a cabin door were opened to the outside, thick fog condensed in the ship's corridors, forming ice and ruining damp bedding. Fog and cigarette smoke hung in the air, enveloping the ship, encircling the crew. Officers played skittles in scarves and great coats, their hands trembling with every move.

Cold is the condition, but wind the disease. Few words in the Viking language remain but those for wind do: *gro* (wind), *stoor* (slight breeze), *gooster* (strong breeze), *daggastoo* (wet wind), *guzzel* (a dry, parching March wind), *pirr* (light wind in July or August), *ungass* (contrary wind), *flann* (tornadolike winds). Winds of more than one hundred and seventy knots rip over islands in the North Atlantic, lifting men from their feet and over cliffs, wrenching babies from the arms of mothers. Walls are several feet thick on the windward side. When the flanns blow, it's pure fury behind four walls.

In the north, wind propels snow and ice like gunshot. Even the staunchest sons of Empire with the most prodigious bladders must take cover.

We moved to my Uncle Bill's house across the road from Franklin foundry after my uncle lost his job in the Noma lights factory, an American-owned plant that in one year closed all its Canadian operations. Uncle Bill had worked on the line where lights were molded into Disney characters, German folk figurines, and English cottages. He used to work Saturday mornings at the factory outlet. We'd get glass Plutos, Billy Goat Gruffs, and long-stemmed bubble lights for free. The week the plant closed, everyone bought Christmas lights at reduced rates, even the premium ones for export, and houses in Keppel glowed in amber, blue and red like never before.

When my uncle left to find a job in Toronto, he took with him my cousins, Debbie, Donna, and Dell, and Aunt Iris, my mother's sister. Then my father moved us from the apartment house into my uncle's house. We took on all their furnishings, including stacks of *Fave Rave* magazines, pinups of Elvis and Troy Donahue, shiny black towers of 45s and 78s that we weren't allowed to touch, and Grandfather, who lived in a room off the front door.

No matter how much Grandfather would pat down his gray hair it would never lie flat. Bits of fuzz from his orange-brown cardigan clung to his flannel trousers. From my perch on the raised footstool of his La-Z-Boy, I watched him through the burgundy glass of the ashtray he kept on an ornate brass stand and listened to his adventures in South Africa, where as sergeant-major he kept the peace for a tour of duty. Then my favorite story, of how he was shot and wounded in a foxhole somewhere in France. Here, trace the scar, he'd say. Tinted burgundy, his muscled arm seemed years younger, the forearm of a fighting man, and I loved to touch it. Hard and smooth, peeled birchbark come to life. Bone fragments had lodged in his forearm above the elbow, and when I'd do as I was told and pressed the hard lumps, his arm sprung up in mock salute. Then we'd laugh and laugh.

Across the road, boy, Grandfather would say, those Franklin propellers will soon be on the open sea. They'll be taking cargo to London, around the Cape of Good Hope, to India, Ceylon, the South Seas. Soldiers had heard Keppel was a proper place for working men, and many had booked passage there after the War. Grandfather was a cabinet maker before the War; in Keppel he built dressing tables and bureaus for families who were arriving by the boatload. At that time the town was a shipbuilding center and transshipment point for wheat and barley that came from the West. But with the opening of the St. Lawrence Seaway, larger ships than ever before could voyage nonstop from Lake Superior to the Atlantic, and ports like Keppel's were no longer necessary. Grandfather didn't know and I never told him that the building and opening of the Seaway had made redundant the propellers for the size of ships that Franklin's once built, that the sound that woke me every day in my uncle's house was not that of workers building parts for giant ships but of welders making trash bins for apartments in Toronto.

Father, on the other hand, seemed not to notice me when we lived in my uncle's house. If it is an age-old fantasy of men to disappear, to leave wives and kids for kicking stones on the open road, Father was a rank failure as a man. He never wanted to go anywhere. He could have lived alone in the basement, feeding logs into the airtight, miter-cutting baseboard strips, or picking over scrap nails he kept in old Miracle Whip jars whose lids he'd hammered into a two-by-four on the ceiling.

He did play with me in those years in my uncle's house. Catch. I was seven years old and still sucking my thumb. It seemed to me the most natural thing in all the world. The thumb in your mouth. In church, in the stands above the softball diamond, in the back seat of the family car. Suck and draw yourself inside. Harder and harder. The thumb is useless as a finger. Eventually the thumb takes on the shape and color of the inside of the mouth. Red, splotchy. Soft and getting softer, so soft it might just disappear. Up and inside and gone.

"C'mon, boy," Father said that day. "I got a surprise for you." Father, with his hands behind his back, ordered me to pick one, and I did. To my surprise, he was holding a gift: A brand-new baseball glove. Something for my thumb. "If you stop sucking your thumb," he said, "this will be yours to keep. Now let's play catch." In his other hand was a Black Diamond glove, a real catcher's mitt, heavily padded.

Then he whipped a softball toward me. I managed to catch every pitch he threw that day, but with each one I felt my thumb bend back a little more. Still I didn't call out or tell him to stop. Once, when he drilled the ball at me, the glove flew off, and I shook my hand in pain. My father laughed, seemed pleased with himself. I said nothing to answer his laughter, nothing when he asked me if I was all right between laughs. He did not come close enough to see my thumb swelling, turning from red to black and blue. Life was a test of wills, I thought. Sometimes fathers must hurt their sons. Take life as it comes. Go along to get along. Later, I would be clapped on the shoulder, "Atta Boy." Then, alone, pack the bruises in ice. Throbbing inside the glove, the thumb was ugly, suddenly adult.

Grandfather and Father didn't like each other, but as near as I could tell, Father never showed Grandfather his mean side. He grumbled at Grandfather's passive style of card-playing, at the smell of his pipe he smoked once an evening. Worse, on Saturday nights, Grandfather staked out his La-Z-Boy in the best spot for watching *Hockey Night in Canada* on TV. Grandfather rooted for Stan Mikita and Bobby Hull and the Chicago Blackhawks, never the Toronto Maple Leafs, my father's team. Still, they didn't speak angrily to one another or even raise their voices. Open confrontation—a thrown ashtray, a screaming fight—was unheard of. An angry outburst in my father's house would be as likely as a French kiss at a church social.

Like father, I'd slip away. Once I left Uncle Stan's house, where our family was visiting. It was autumn. In a Keppel autumn the sound of feet shuffling fallen leaves quakes the soul. The sound of rusting rakes on pavement, bent tines twanging in the crisp air. The day I fled my uncle's house I lay still in our backyard, deep in the leaves, completely covered, soothed by the rustle of the maple, elm, and oak leaves rising and falling with my shallow breaths. First, Father came. He thought I was hiding inside the house and banged the screen door, calling for me to come out this instant. If you know what's good for you, boy, you'll come out here right now. I know you're in here. Each call stabbed like a pitchfork, my gut bleeding fear. He'll find me out here, shake me so my teeth hurt, so the back of my head explodes. But then, he was gone and Mum came. She stood in the backyard and was quiet. On some deep level she was aware. On a pure fall day a child can no more hide from his mother in a pile of leaves than he can fly to the moon. I will let him alone, let his father's anger cool, she thought. Then she, too, went away. At last Grandfather reached into the leaves and pulled me out. He hugged me and told me it would be all right. No, Grampa, I said, it won't be all right. Come back into the leaves with me. Lie down in the leaves with me and tell me the truth.

If it were not for the cold, hundreds of passengers aboard the *Titanic* would have lived. On the day of the accident, the weather was fine, the sea calm. All one thousand four hundred and eighty-nine passengers who entered the frigid water that day were dead when the rescue ship reached them less than two hours later. Nineteen pages of death notices incorrectly cited drowning as the cause of death. Most died of the cold.

In "The Little Match Girl," by Hans Christian Andersen, a girl who had been trying to sell matches all day stopped to rest by the roadside. She had lost her shoes, and her thin, ragged clothes were wet from snow that had been falling heavily. The girl was tired and hungry, and the smells of cooking coming from houses aggravated her hunger. As night fell, she curled into a ball and tried to sleep but was too cold. She struck one of the matches, and in the flame of it she saw a stove with a roaring fire. When the match went out, she lit another and saw in its flame a table groaning with food that she could almost taste. She imagined a Christmas tree with candles in the third match, and when it disappeared she looked up to where the candles had been and saw the stars. The flame of the fourth match grew large as she saw the beloved face of her former protector, her grandmother, who had died that year. She was so afraid that her grandmother too would disappear once again that she struck match after match until eventually the old woman took the girl in her arms and soared into the heavens. The Little Match Girl was found dead the next day from hypothermia, with a saintly smile on her face.

Those in the throes of hypothermia have hallucinated like The Little Match Girl, seen visions of sides of roast beef, a Sasquatch in the forest, a gentle grandparent long-dead. The spirit the Algonquins call Windigo—a mythic beast with a heart of ice—has long preyed on the imagination. More than two thousand years ago, Herodotus wrote of a Persian fleet wrecked by a northerly gale in which twenty thousand sailors died: "Some were seized and devoured by sea monsters, while others were dashed violently against the rocks; some who did not know how to swim were engulfed and some died of cold." In modern wartime, the majority of soldiers killed at sea died of hypothermia, not drowning. And although medicine has begun to control cold with good results (by putting patients into deep hypothermia, surgeons can regulate the flow of blood to the brain and conduct sophisticated brain and heart operations), it's still common that causes of death in water are attributed to drowning without the temperature of the body ever being taken.

Hallucinations follow the first stages of hypothermia. Victims become uncooperative, shiver uncontrollably. The mind dims and the shivering stops before amnesia occurs. Those in deep hypothermia, 80.6°F, may be indistinguishable from the dead: skin icy to the touch, body temperature low, muscles and joints stiff, heartbeat inaudible. At 68°F the heart stops.

"Answer never a word/For a frozen corpse was he," Longfellow wrote. Death by freezing is said to be painless, gradual, and slow; the secret to staying alive is to keep moving. Fingers freeze easily so they must be protected and beaten on the body to restore circulation if they begin feeling numb. Toes and feet are also susceptible, but people have been known to walk up to three full days on frozen feet. It is like "skimming the earth," says the man who froze to death in Jack London's short story "To Build a Fire." But once the fingers go the rest will follow. Wits begin to wander and exhaustion descends. Sleep swallows you whole and you lie down in the snow and freeze.

Sit next to me, Father said. Be my good luck charm. When Grandfather lived with us, Mum's family often visited. In the evening they would play cards, six-handed euchre or "Bug Your Neighbor." Never hearts. I'd sit next to Father and first he would whisper to me, say he was going to trump this trick, slough off the next. But soon he'd forget about me and be immersed in the game, snapping cards on the Formica, grumbling when a jack was overtrumped, when he kept the wrong ace. I'd pray for his luck to hold. Deliver unto Father aces, face cards in the trump suits, scotch the wee ones, the threes and fours. Let me just sit here on my hands, dear God, and watch. But it was no use. Soon everyone would be sitting back on their chairs, giving Father more room. Yellow lampshades and burgundy-tinted glass blurred the light while my aunts and uncles sucked cigarettes and drank highballs from plastic glasses and Father drained all the air from the room.

Before long I'd excuse myself and go play the hand of Grandfather, who spread the cards before me like a silk fan. Through the smoke I could see my father, fanning his cards as if it were a signal to me. I'll get even with you. You'll see, boy, you cannot defy me. I froze and could not go to him. Even when his luck turned and he won, when he was smiling and telling how he had done it, when he was raking in his winnings of quarters, nickels, and dimes, the chill in his eyes kept me away.

And then one day, Grandfather was gone. He was on his way to Toronto to live with Uncle Bill. It happened so suddenly; even the portrait in his parade uniform and the heavy glass ashtray and stand were left behind. Mum said there was not enough room in the place where we were to move, and that Grandfather would be well taken care of in Toronto. But I didn't believe her. Grandfather would never have willingly left Keppel. I was sure it was Father's idea. "So long, boy," Grandfather said, smelling of tobacco and felt. "Take care." Then he left for Toronto.

Father never told me stories. When he bought a couch for the living room he answered my question of how much it cost with the expression "Money and thanks." But Grandfather told tales of northern explorers and army life in distant lands. Those times with him at the house near the foundry were my first happy memories.

In our new house, a two-story insul-brick on a dead-end street, there were no more family visits, no card games at the kitchen table. The ashtray and stand were sold, Grandfather's portrait stored away. For months I didn't sleep through the night. Night after night I screwed up my courage and in my pajamas and slippers padded downstairs to the doorway of my parents' bedroom. What did I think I was going to do? Call out to him in the dark? Confront him like a man? Instead, I did nothing. I stood like a ghost before the open door of my parents' bedroom for what seemed like hours, wondering that a boy my age in India had once seen his own father decapitated by murderous raiders, that Abraham was prepared to slay his own son as a sacrifice to God until God told him no, that it was better that he was prepared to do it as an act of faith than to actually do it. Shades of moonlight rose and fell on the bed. Boys were numb, pathetic creatures, nothing more than their fathers' sons, common vessels collecting, drip by drip, the sins of the fathers.

Of course, never did I stand longer than a moment at their doorway. Mum always stirred and woke up. "What is it, son? Are you all right? Can I get you anything? Why are you standing there like that?" Eventually, she told me to go back upstairs, and I returned to bed.

I wish, looking back, that I'd have challenged Father, asked what he wanted of me, defended Grandfather, who'd been sent away. But in my terrible regard of Father I had grown silent like him. I'd grown up with the idea that to be a man you had to take life as it comes. That phantoms that emerged in driveways at night were not to be trusted.

The Tlingit, a tribe from the coldest of lands where the salmon runs, have a saying: Only the dead warm.

When the first Europeans came upon the Tlingit they were huddled around a fire in spare huts. Over them were blankets imbued with the odor of decayed salmon and the resinous smoke of burning spruce and pine. Cold penetrated huts that offered protection from no more than drifting snow and light winds.

A corpse was dressed in glorious raiment so fine that it had been stored away and never been worn. It was said evil spirits lurked by the entranceway of the dead's hut, so the body was carried through an opening in the wall created by removing loose boards, out onto the funeral pyre, where mourners felt the searing heat only on their faces. For more than a week during the celebration of the dead, routines stopped as feasting raged until the entire store of meat was gone.

The Tlingit believed the dead went to an island of plenty across a river of fire, a paradise where it was always warm, where game was good. Death without fire was a shadow in thick, impenetrable frost. The drowned—the blanketless—were doomed to shiver forever.

Every winter until the clean air laws were passed, Keppel burned its Christmas trees. No event was more popular. Itchy Phil Stokes, the town fool, who on Sundays wore a ratty pinstriped suit and wandered church to church to church (but never went inside), solicited snow shovelings at the gate before the mayor and specialty advertiser, Bill Miller, delivered a short speech and free balloons to children, matchbooks to adults. The poor kids ran every which way in the dark, but others, like me, sat on their hands inside cars and under blankets, waiting politely for the speeches to stop and the burning to begin.

On the night of the last bonfire, Father decided to go early to get a good parking spot, close to the mountain of trees. After dinner, he warmed up the car and set out blankets for us. My sister, my brother, and I raced into the bitter cold, jumped into the car, and huddled under the blankets that had been warmed by the car's heater. My mother and father exchanged smiling glances on the way to the burning while we sat toasty and warm in back.

That night Father was in a rare talkative mood. He told us how important it was to heat up the car on nights below zero so the engine wouldn't misfire. We learned how he was expanding his territory as a traveling salesman, selling candy bars and baseball cards "to beat the band," opening accounts with small groceries, promising five-and-dimes. He was on his way to being the most successful salesman in his company. For the past three years he had been the top salesman in confectionery (candy and chewing gum) and now was number three in sundries (big-markup items like toasters and electric shavers). He was doing it all for us . . . the good days were just around the corner . . . we would all be happy.

Father talked, yes, but it wasn't a conversation meant to be entered. As he went on about sales trends and snowblowers, curling draws and commissions, I stopped listening and imagined seeing our own tree in the green thicket before me. We played this game, my family and I, of picking out a tree in the bonfire pile that looked like the tree we had decorated at home. We each picked only one and the winner was declared to be the person whose tree survived the flames the longest. The one that could best withstand the heat.

Finally, Mayor Bill torched the pile. A loud "WOW" rose from the crowd. Those not in cars started clapping, hooting, and hollering. Father, as most fathers did, leaned on the horn. The crackling of the tree limbs, too, was deafening. Soon, the crowd grew silent. Heat pressed down from above like it did from the open door of our coal-burning furnace. Faces glowed red, mouths were agape. Trees burst into flames as the bonfire raged upwards, higher than the treeline, reaching into the heavens.

darkness

An Eskimo hunter can see things in the darkness a white man can't see. In the gray light of an arctic January an Eskimo can kill foxes and hares with a single shot. The white man sees nothing.

It's in darkness, too, in winter, that Eskimos sleep twelve to fifteen hours at a time. During periods of plenty, they live to do nothing more than eat, drink, and sleep under the midnight sun. The best houses are judged by the length of their uninterrupted cycles of eating and sleeping.

From time to time Victorians arrived and lived among the Eskimos. One visitor, a survivor of a foundered whaling ship, once awoke in a large igloo before many Eskimos. The dim flame of the animal oil lamp was not strong enough to read by, so he lay on his back, looking at the rough, uneven sides of the igloo. Slumbering hulks of hunters, their wives, and children filled every corner. An orphan, the boy he'd come to know as the son of the host's dead brother, rose to tend the lamp. The boy blocked the light with his body and the outlines of sleeping figures faded to black.

Surrounding him were people who had never been immersed in hot water. Soup was a vile-smelling liquid swimming with oily globs; other stone pots contained piss and shit. The whaler had once seen an Eskimo girl prepare for a night out by washing her hair in her own piss. He too had not washed for months; but for his height and blue eyes he was indistinguishable from his hosts.

Finally, people stirred. Some were inspecting knife blades, others picking lice from the beards of their neighbors. Dogs whimpered from beyond icy walls. The host slapped his body hard with both hands from head to toe to restore circulation, and others did the same. It was deafening, a symphony of skin. Men yelled at one another, laughed, lunged mockingly with the blunt ends of weapons.

Then a shape on the central sleeping platform emerged from under a pile of caribou and polar bear skins. The first-born son had risen, straight-backed and solemn, like a crown prince at a fraternity party.

One day not long after Grandfather died, Father put a portrait of a woman on top of the television set. She had my father's round face with dark brown eyes, hair like cotton batting, and a thin smile. Black dress, beads, pearl clasp earrings. Glasses.

"Who's that?" I asked. The *Rocky and Bullwinkle Show* was on. Moose antlers sprouted in a cornfield. "Who's that woman, Dad?"

Father blanched as he turned to leave to go back to his worktable. As quiet as he was, he was never tongue-tied when spoken to. But this time he didn't meet my gaze—he just put a finger to his lips and walked unsteadily toward me and the living room exit. He appeared not to hear me when I called out loudly after him, "Who's in the picture, Dad?" as if to a cartoon image, an elderly man with a horn to his ear. I could hear his footsteps on the basement stairs as he descended to his tangle of wires and wood studs. I rose to get a closer look at the dignified-looking woman in a frame on the television set.

In times of famine, prayers to the Maiden of the Deep go unanswered, and for weeks on end little game is caught. Orphans and those who are declared unproductive are not fed at all. Elders wander off.

Once long ago a beautiful Eskimo girl, Teulijuk, spent her waking hours not helping her mother with clothes-making and mending but combing her own long, lustrous hair. Her father implored Teulijuk to help her mother but the stubborn girl refused. While the father hunted for seals and the mother mended clothing, the girl sat on the sleeping platform in the igloo combing her hair.

When the young men of the village learned that Teulijuk was not eager to do what was expected of a woman they did not come by, and soon others neglected the family igloo. Teulijuk listened to her parents' pleas to help around the house, but she did not change her ways.

One day the parents took Teulijuk out in the water aboard a boat, and when they were in the middle of a deep channel threw her overboard. She went under but managed to cling to the boat's side, pleading for mercy. Between the two of them they could not break her hold, so the father took an axe and chopped off her hands.

But the people were not to be rid of Teulijuk so easily. Her spirit remains on the ocean floor, gathering creatures of the deep in her once-beautiful hair, a fabulous flutter in the icy current. Without fingers she can't comb out these tresses, so the meat that would otherwise be caught and sustain the people remains with Teulijuk, the Maiden of the Deep, who is taking her revenge, keeping food from them all.

In the new house, looking at photographs and making drawings were my sole acts of rebellion. After dinner we were herded before the television set, told to hush when the evening programs started. If the phone rang it was often for me, and I left the room without a sound, like an acolyte stealing away from a ceremony. In our house, where TV took the place of conversation and storytelling, all other activities were subversive. After talking briefly on the phone, I'd sneak upstairs and look at photos.

The pictures were jammed into a brown and white shoe box kept on the second floor in a cubbyhole—a tiny closet latched by a piece of wood no bigger than my thumb. The door to the space was the only one in the house I would never leave open. I opened doors but never closed them. It was the same with lights. They went on but not off. Once Mum returned home to find every light on and the front and back doors and every interior door—to rooms, cupboards, cabinets, even drawers—open. She reproached me for such waste and inattentiveness, but I was incredulous. Indeed, could not remember that I had done such a thing. Even today I leave doors half-open, lights on. Anyone who has lived in the silence of secrets and lies is forever on a mission.

In the dappled light of the cubbyhole, I sat cross-legged among discarded baby clothes, baseball cards, comic books, an Eaton's catalogue. With the hairs of my head touching the ceiling, my elbows at the wall, I pored over old photos and began sketching, making little pencil drawings of what I found. I sat with my ear pressed against the smooth white door of the cubbyhole, half-listening for the sound of Father's footsteps on the stairs.

In most photographs—holding my sister who had just pissed her overalls through and through, in a bathing suit mugging Lauren Bacall, at work, wearing the headphones of a Bell operator—my mother had a crooked smile. Hearing the expression, "Cheese!" Mum's upper lip would tremble and twitch, her eyelids droop. In some shots it looked like the left side of her face was paralyzed; in others she appeared devious, wanton, like a gangster's moll.

In one she looked natural, not nervous at all. She was wearing her full-length beaver coat, which I loved to sneak a touch of when she took it off beside me on the pew at church. She and Father were standing atop the largest snowbank I had ever seen, up to their knees in snow. Both were smiling so hard I was sure they'd burst. I think that if the picture were in color their faces would have been beet red, as red as they could be.

Two adults who looked something like my mother and father appeared in a passionate embrace in another photo. I had never seen my parents together in such a way, kissing, like lovers. The picture was dark and shadowy, the romantic mood deliberate. The woman appeared to be part of the lanky handsome man—in his arms, a light hue, crushed fabric. Her hair was tousled, fuzzy in the half-light, hinting movement. The photo's center was the man's neck, the top of the woman's head. In the background a car was parked.

It seemed to me that the couple was doing something forbidden; something terrible that they were ashamed of, that they would come to regret. I came to believe that those lovers—the night they kissed so hard before a photographer, the night a sedan was parked nearby, the night the light was right—were on the run.

Eskimos fear the spirit of the earth, hunger, and sickness; and they fear souls—those both of people and animals, killed and living.

When Knud Rasmussen, the Eskimo ethnographer, once asked the people about their faith, he was met with silence. Few outsiders had earned the people's trust as Rasmussen had, yet he, too, was denied. Finally, an elder agreed to talk to him. They stood on a windswept coast as the men of the camp returned without game from a day of hunting seal on the ice. "Why?" the old man asked. Rasmussen said nothing. The elder took him into an igloo where a woman and a young man shivered before a flickering flame of a lamp. "Why?" the old man asked again, and then explained that their hunter had brought home no game. Next they went to an igloo where an old woman lay alone, sick with hunger. The man asked Rasmussen again, "Why?" Each time, Rasmussen made no reply.

"You are unable to give any reason when we ask you why life is as it is," said the elder. "And so it must be. All our customs come from life and turn toward life; we explain nothing, we believe nothing, but in what I have shown you lies our answer to all you ask."

Fear commands the living not to pronounce aloud the name of the dead until the spirit it bears can be passed on to a newborn child. Survivors cry for only a brief time and console themselves with the word *Iyonamut* ("It can't be helped, there's no changing it").

Then they sing:

> I am afraid
> When my eyes follow the moon
> On its old trail.

> I am afraid
> When I hear the wind wailing
> And the murmuring of snow.

> I am afraid
> When I watch the stars
> Moving on their nightly trails.

> I am afraid.
—Anon

When the nights are longest, women suffering from *perlerorneq*—the disease of darkness—eat dog dung, shred caribou hides of family clothing, howl at the moon. Numb with fear, children huddle in the corner of the igloo. Eskimos say that to thwart *perlerorneq* it is best not to indulge in free-thinking. Better to live each day as it comes; to hunt if a man, sew clothes if a woman. To think is to bring on the disease.

Once a northern woman was named the leader of her people. With a great sense of duty, she began in her role by listening to white men, who told her that she must lead the people from the land of her ancestors to a place they had never seen. She was told white men had special purposes for the sacred land. The people were promised that their new home would be bountiful. After much talk of this kind, she spoke for the people and consented to the move.

The land they were taken to was barren, the game poor, and even healthy people began to grow sick and die. White men told the woman leader that an unfortunate mistake was made, that there was a better land ahead, that they would be taken there. But she said the people wouldn't have moved the first time if they had known the white men would lie to them. They didn't want to go to this new place, they wanted to return home. The white men said going home was impossible, that the land of their ancestors was no longer theirs. The woman said white men are nothing but lies.

She was against it but the people were moved again. In this new land they were trained to fish with line, lures, and poles. But they had never lived on such food. Here too they began to die. That winter the woman leader caught *perlerorneq*, and in a fit took a club and beat to near-death several Eskimo men. She tore down shacks, destroyed racks where fish were drying, and was ripping into and spoiling caches of food when she was finally stopped by her own people, by two men who killed her to save themselves.

But the white men did not see it as a killing in self-defense. To them, a woman—a person with whom they had established a trust—had been murdered by nameless men. Two Eskimos were charged with murder, tried by a court, and punished with years of imprisonment. For the lost people who dream of home only sentences are served.

There was nothing special about the exterior of my father's cedar chest on the second floor. Except for the rounded edge on the top, it was square, with a dark wood border along the base. I knew the chest was Father's because he used the copper key on his key ring to open it. He didn't do it often, but about the time he placed the picture of the woman on the television set, Father came upstairs late at night and opened the chest. On winter nights the bedroom doors were always open because the only source of heat was a single register in the hall, and from my bed at the window I could see the chest and my father kneeling before it.

The first few times I saw him I thought I was dreaming. Leaning over the cedar chest, his hands deep inside, my father was a greedy pirate, then a pious priest. I could see only the underside of the chest's lid. Never had I seen the contents.

What could be in there? I thought of books and diaries, but there was never much to read in my father's house. Father looked at *Reader's*

Digest and the local paper, and Mum read *Reader's Digest* and kept clippings from the bridge column in the *Illustrated Bible*. On the floor of the cubbyhole was a red, shiny, bound edition of *Reader's Digest* with a game inside of buccaneers and hidden treasure that I liked to play, and a blue hardcover edition of *Robinson Crusoe*. But that was it for books. Instead, I imagined the chest held keepsakes—a baby's bootie, a sailor's suit, a slingshot—clues to Father's past. A birth certificate or letters from his family. Perhaps Father was having affairs and kept pictures of women he met on the road, their love letters, or letters from an old flame.

Once the covers rustled as I moved a bit in bed to get a better look, and Father whipped around, cut me an angry stare. "Are you awake?" he said in a voice like planed gravel. I didn't move, kept my breathing even, closed my eyes shut. Keep still, I thought. Soon he would turn back to the chest, convinced that I was asleep. But for what seemed an eternity I felt the steady pressure of him. He had crept up to me, would strike me with a closed fist. I trembled with the thought, tensed for the blow. But it didn't come. Eventually, I opened my eyes to slits again and saw him back before the open chest.

I felt many things on those nights but fear was the strongest, and it kept me from calling out to him. Fear that if I did interrupt him he would punish me, spank me as he did when I misbehaved. Perhaps worse.

Earlier that summer he'd scared me as he never had before. Like most kids, I liked to be buried in sand at the beach. I'd seen it on television, on *The Monkees*. I got into a hole in the earth and then Father packed the sand around me. My arms were straight to my side. Cool grains of sand pressed against me from my toes to the hollow of my throat. "You'll be okay, son," Father said before leaving to go swim in the lake. "We'll see you later." There were no spectators—only bird tracks, windblown husks, dead pine needles. My head sprouted like an asparagus—remote, alone and exotic.

Hard sand beneath my feet, pressed against my flesh, entering every pore. Then, suddenly, I couldn't breathe. My arms couldn't move, my feet only dug in deeper.

I was losing consciousness when Baby Bruce, a little cousin of mine, slammed shut the screen door. "Bruce," I said. "Go get someone to help." Bruce stopped and stared, held my gaze for a long time and then I blacked out.

The people in the cottage who were too drunk to swim must have heeded Baby Bruce because the next thing I knew I was on a vinyl sofa, wrapped in towels, my armpits aching from being yanked out of a hole in the ground. An uncle's anxious-looking face hovered above me; Father, as always, was nowhere to be seen.

Once Father really did lose it. I was visiting a friend and my father came to pick me up. Before we left, my friend challenged Father to a game of ping pong. The game was close at first, a point's margin either way. Then my friend stepped up the tempo, sending balls on service with top spin, smashing volleys. Father was an out-of-work samurai, flailing away. At game point the boy had won thirteen straight and Father, breathing heavily, looked like a madman, his eyes black and menacing. "Look out!" I screamed as the paddle went flying out of Father's hand toward the face of the boy. He ducked and the paddle smashed against the wall. Then Father grabbed me roughly by the shoulder and pulled me out of there.

I was afraid of his temper, but the thought that he would never return to the cedar chest was a worse fear. Father's nightly visits were the only clue I had ever had to his secret life, his past that remained a mystery to me. Faking sleep on those nights that Father knelt before the cedar chest, I resolved to take the risk, to find out more about him on my own.

In earlier years, I had stood on that chest and leaped to the floor, imagining myself a caped crusader. I had knelt before it, my teeth gnawing through the varnish to the soft wood, chewing an "L" before Mum shooed me away. I'd thought that my father's cedar chest was a mere object to serve me. I had no idea until Father began these nightly visits that I was wrong. That somehow the chest had power over me.

I had never done anything to anger Father, to risk unleashing the rage within. But this seemed worth the risk.

Northerners were once called cannibals who worshipped the sun, so little was known of them. When the first Europeans came upon Eskimos eating raw meat on a frozen wasteland they believed the food was human flesh because they could not see how the Eskimos could survive and not eat their own kind.

Yet Eskimos are not cannibals; or at least no more so than anyone else. When a plane carrying a Uruguayan soccer team crashed in the Andes, survivors lived because they ate their dead. More than a century ago, the *New York Times* devoted its front page to the news that six of the original twenty-five members of the renowned Greely Expedition to the north were still alive. But celebration turned to horror and disgust when it was discovered that two men—both of whom were not among the survivors—had stayed alive by cannibalizing some of the deceased. After verifying these findings, Congress voted to suspend publicly funded expeditions to the Arctic. The north itself had driven them mad, a senator said.

Southerners on vessels stuck for long winters in northern ice never learned about food and surviving from the Eskimos. Sick with scurvy, these sailors grew listless, found getting up from bed difficult, strained. Those who managed to rise angered easily and were unable to do even the simplest tasks without tiring. The salted food they ate gave them no energy, no relief from the lethargy; and driven by panic they often stole such food, thinking wrongly that by eating more they would get better. Sores from the lashes they received as punishment for stealing didn't heal. Gums turned spongy and bled openly as teeth loosened and fell out in their hands or clattered on the deck.

Even at this late stage of the disease, the men would have recovered in the care of Eskimos. They would have been force-fed the blood of fresh kill—seals, bears, and walruses—and then later given fresh meat. But Eskimos were regarded as savages, no better than animals, and their wisdom was not sought out. Aboard their own ships the sailors soon didn't have the strength to rise from their beds. Breath stank to high heaven, and in unspeakable pain they writhed in their own piss and shit and died.

On weekends Father used to hang his main set of keys by the back door on a wooden replica of an outsize key he had cut on his jigsaw. He'd take only the car keys to the golf course on Saturdays and Sundays, leaving the other ones at home.

One Saturday morning when Helen and Jim were watching cartoons and my mother was staring out the kitchen window at a neighbor's garden, I sneaked out to the back room to get the keys. I could hear every creak in the floorboards, so I balanced myself on the top edge of the wide baseboards that ran the perimeter of the back room. Tight against the walls, my fingernails gripping the panel siding, I walked along the top of the baseboards until I got to the door. Breathless, I took the keys.

I took the stairs two at a time and soon I was kneeling before the chest just as I had watched my father do so many times before. I felt as if I were back in the sandhole: gasping and afraid. Behind me I could feel my father's eyes, and I looked around to see nothing, only the open door of my bedroom.

The worn copper key slipped easily into the lock. Suddenly I thought I should stop, turn back and return the keys to the hook. I could live with my father as a fictional character, an orphan, a mystery man. What if he were a fugitive, someone who had swindled or killed someone? Somebody like me, deceptive, leading a double life?

The key turned and the lid opened. Rich smells of cedar swept over me. Inside were faded manila folders, rectangular shapes wrapped in brown paper, shoe boxes of old receipts. I touched a scuffed-up baseball, held an old postcard of a main street in the Prairies, a seagull feather that I thought to take but didn't dare.

There was a snapshot of a little girl. She wore a black crinoline dress with a white, wide-brimmed collar of long ago. Her hand, engulfed by the frill of the sleeve, showed only the tips of fingers holding a wicker chair that was three times her size. Blond ringlets flowed to her waist; chubby cheeks nudged thin smile lines. The photograph was old yet the image was sharp, suggesting careful handling, even love. Looking at her I thought that she had the same simple smile of the portrait my father had placed weeks before on top of the television set.

In a shoe box near the picture were faded envelopes stuffed with news clippings. Dark headlines on yellowed paper. I reached in to get a closer look, but heard the back door slam and carefully closed the lid to listen. Friends had arrived, were on their way up. I closed and locked the cedar chest and met my friends on the stairs. Later, I told myself, I'd check it out later, as I put the keys back where they belonged. But when I returned to the door after my playmates had left, the keys were gone.

i c e

Ice takes time, many years, for snow crystals to become almost spherical, for bonds between crystals to form. What results is firn, the intermediate stage between snow and glacial ice. In some northern places, firnballs, not snowballs, are thrown. On impact they scatter in thousands of sparkling fragments. The packing is not good. If you lie down in firn, an impression isn't made. Never an angel.

The first member of my father's family whom I ever saw was holding an orange SLOW sign in a road crew. I was older then, about fourteen. Father was driving Mum and me in the company car down a country road on the way to Uncle Stan's cottage. If Jim and Helen were there, I don't remember.

When we joined the long line of traffic, waves of heat rose from metal and asphalt. Up ahead stretched vehicles like ours, with kids in the back seat, beach balls rolling in station wagons. A line of cars in Keppel can inch ahead for miles on end, their drivers patiently waiting for traffic to clear. Never do they wave their fists in anger or honk their horns in exasperation. In Keppel, to be in line is a passive thing, a fact of life, a duty; in New York, one is on line, active, pressing for an advantage. Bored by the silence and sweaty in the heat, I slumped on the green cloth of the back seat as the car crept along.

When Mum said it was a work crew that was causing the delay, and I sat up again and saw in the distance a person in a brilliant orange vest holding a sign that said SLOW in large letters. The sign girl wore white shorts, a red T, sunglasses, and Greb construction boots. She had a dark tan. Her legs were shapely, slightly muscled, her arms long and slender for her height. Jet black hair, a bob cut, the style of the day. Perfect white teeth flashed as she smiled our way and Father smiled back and winked. I had never seen a more beautiful girl in a road crew.

"Wasn't that Mary back there?" Mum asked, turning toward Father.

"Huh?" Father said, cutting his eyes at Mum. "What are you talking about?"

"Your niece, Mary. I . . ."

"Nah," my father said. "Couldn't be."

In the direct sunlight of the open road, Mary's skin was the color of brown sugar. She flipped the sign from SLOW to STOP and then cars blocked the view.

"C'mon Dad, for real? My cousin?" I cried, pounding the armrest.

Father glared at me in the rearview mirror. "Could be, I guess," he said. His eyes seemed to be sinking deep into his sockets, gradually, like heated stones on ice. "I suppose it could be."

Perhaps it was because I had turned fourteen, was growing up. Or maybe it had something to do with my cousin, the sign girl. But that summer Father began to reveal something about himself. During Sunday drives to the beach, Father looked at Cousin Mary's brown legs and curved hips, then told us stories about a boy's life on a farm.

Perhaps Mum had had some premonition about Mary and me falling in love and getting married, both of us ignorant of our roots. She'd waited until I was older to tip me off, to reveal the secret about my cousin Mary and save us from ourselves, from making an unforgivable mistake. I imagined that long ago Father had had a feud with his brother, who lived with his wife and children on a farm, one that had been in the family for generations. Father had been disinherited, thrown out years ago after a bitter disagreement. The bad feelings between the two of them had something to do with the way, when he thought no one was looking, he gave Mary the eye. Father was a rake; a bad seed.

But Father's stories weren't about that. It was as if the stories had been rehearsed, like lines a would-be immigrant practices to be accepted in the new world, revealing so little of himself, only what is necessary.

"I worked on a farm, but I didn't make the kind of money your cousin Mary here does," he said, jerking his outstretched thumb toward the road crew. "Mary, she holds that sign eight hours a day, five days a week, and for any overtime is paid eight dollars an hour. During haying alone, I worked fifteen hours a day, seven days a week. If I got five bucks I was lucky."

I imagined the sweltering heat in the hayloft at the farm where my father worked as a boy. Some days were so hot he glistened in sweat. Small for his age, Father worked in tight spots on farm machinery that men could not reach, fashioning strong hands and wrists from turning stubborn bolts and gaining a knack with wood. In the evenings he helped with the building of tool sheds, supply houses, worked his way up to home repair.

"I quit school the summer I was your age, and for four summers I worked on this farm. It belonged to a neighbor, a good man, never treated me badly."

In the bunkhouse for hired hands, the flies never let up. When I was growing up, friends of my mother's had farms, and I'd go there. Farm boys I'd played with didn't flinch when houseflies lit on the backs of their hands. It was the same with ants, which in summer crawled from the smooth wooden counters onto their arms, then back to the counters again. As a fourteen-year-old boy, my father— flies buzzing about his head—fell fast asleep each night in the bunkhouse for working men, never straining for sleep.

But then, too, I think it was not like that. In his stories of farm life, the hardness of it, of how tossing hundred-pound hay bales had shaped muscular forearms that for years did nothing but push a pencil across order books and raise a two-by-four to a circular saw,

I see something else. I see my father, a little boy in the fields, sweat pouring down his arms, his face red with exertion, struggling to keep up with the men ahead of him, running away from something he cannot face. In the evening he dumps the brackish water of yellow seeds and dying leaves from the hollow of a tire swing and stands on the tire for hours, holding the rope that's attached to the tree. At night he turns his head against the rough-hewn board of the bunkhouse, near the men who are breathing heavily in sleep, and cries for a long, long time.

In Keppel, deep in fissures of the earth, ice of ages lies. Crevices plunge deep into the rocky ground of the Niagara Escarpment, which was formed when a glacier receded ten thousand years ago, exposing a steep rock face that was once the shore of an ancient sea. Atop the escarpment, forests and waterfalls, some appearing on cliffs a thousand feet high, were once home to a forgotten tribe of peace-loving Indians known as the Neutrals, and then to Scottish pioneers, dour settlers who cut bush and farmed the hardscrabble land along the four-hundred-and-fifty-mile expanse toward Manitoulin, the world's largest island in fresh water.

Some crevices are wide enough to fall into, with ledges at their mouth and smooth-looking sides; others are gouges no wider than a man's leg. As a boy, I'd sit before them. I was signed up for swimming lessons, but I didn't go. Instead I went alone and climbed to the top of the escarpment that everyone called "The Rocks."

I liked especially to rest before one large crevice from which frigid air blew. I would shut my eyes and dream of falling in. I grasped icicles and icy ledges, felt the cold of the descent, especially on my face. But I was not alarmed. I felt swathed in the cold, strangely comforted.

For years I visited that crevice until the night I heard a cry for help. The moan of a wounded animal, I thought, calling out in the pitch black as I sat with friends on the cliff.

No one else moved from the circle of young men drinking alcohol mixed with soft drinks from wineskins and Javex bottles, so I thought that the frightened call was for me alone. Slowly I walked in the night until the sound grew louder, then staggered blindly in haste over rocks and tree stumps. Suddenly, inexplicably, I stopped. Gazing down at my feet I saw that the cries were from the shape of a boy, one of us who must have wandered away. He lay crumpled like a rag doll where he had fallen a short distance down the mouth of my crevice and onto a narrow ledge. If I had gone one step farther I would have fallen, too; I would have landed on him and knocked him down with me into the chasm below.

Later, a boy with a rope helped retrieve the fallen one, and the next day at school he wore a sling on his arm and a head bandage, but otherwise he was fine.

I have never been afraid of floods, lightning storms, or blizzard whiteouts. For me, the violence, with every bit of force as that which comes from the skies, has always risen from within.

For a century men traveled to the ice, nearly ecstatic in their willingness to die. When Sir Ernest Shackleton sought volunteers for his ill-fated voyage to Antarctica, he wrote in a London newspaper:

"Men wanted for hazardous journey. Small wages, bitter cold, long months of complete darkness, constant danger, safe return doubtful. Honor and recognition in case of success." Hundreds applied.

Unlike other geographies whose secrets are unraveled through experiment and deduction, ice has kept its mysteries locked away. Stephen J. Pyne, in his book *The Arctic*, calls ice the "geography of nihilism. . . . The ice absorbs, it doesn't emanate."

There is magic, too. The luminists of the nineteenth-century art world arrived to draw the ice, to capture the colors, the blue, green, carmine, and lake. Frederic Church called icebergs the best example of light in nature. His oil *Icebergs* sold at auction in New York in 1979 for $2.9 million, at the time the highest price paid in North America for a painting. Photographs by Scottish artist Andy Goldsworthy of four ice sculptures surrounding the North Pole fetch tens of thousands of dollars for the set. Centuries ago the monks who rowed curraghs for Brendan the Navigator through passageways in giant icebergs were amazed, said they felt as if they had gone through the "Eye of God."

In recent years a secret or two has been unlocked. Scientists have found by drilling almost two miles into Greenland ice that climates have not always changed as slowly as in modern times. From studies of ice layers they have concluded that hippos once swam in the Thames, that lions prowled its shore. Cold has changed in dramatic ways, too, shifting 18°F worldwide in a period of time as short as a couple of decades. During one period, the average global temperature plunged 25°F to Ice Age levels and remained in deep freeze for the next seventy years. Then it became warm again. The cycle of extreme heat and bitter cold continued for another two hundred thousand years, until the last ten thousand years, when the global climate became oddly stable. No one knows why the world has not frozen over in historic time.

I don't remember ever hearing my father laugh harder than when the newspaper boy, Mug Grunwald, teased him about the snow pumpkin crop.

One Saturday, Mug, his paper bag draped over his shoulder, stopped before my father, who was busy shoveling snow from the front lane of the house.

"So, tell me, how are the snow pumpkins coming along?" Mug asked my father.

"What's that?" Father said, pushing his tuque from his eyes as he turned to face Mug.

"The SNOW pumpkins!" Mug cried.

Snow was falling lightly and my father's black eyebrows were dusted white. He was resting on his scoop like Ken Dryden used to do on his goalstick, staring down ice, waiting for the play to come his way.

"How's the harvest coming, the snow pumpkin harvest?" Mug asked, his arms outstretched, acting exasperated. "Everybody has been following your progress—planting, spraying, and now harvesting. I've been coming by every night, admiring your work. Actually, I'd like to take one home tonight, if I could. I've promised my mother a homegrown snow pumpkin . . ."

Father started to laugh. He laughed so hard and loud and long that we all heard him in the house. Hardly able to believe our eyes, we gathered at the kitchen window and watched as Father doubled over in laughter.

"Here," my father said, handing an imaginary snow pumpkin to my new friend. "For your mother."

Hockey is mastery on the surface, the organized aspect of ice. The perfect Canadian game.

I am alone, freshly scrubbed and in white flannel pajamas before a TV set. Davey Keon of the Toronto Maple Leafs flipped the puck from center ice high in the air, a clearing shot. The puck lands, bounces, changes shape—a saucer—then disappears, hits again, harder this time, and higher, higher over an outstretched glove. He shoots! He scores!

The best hockey players have this way of waiting. Gretzky had it; the Bobbys, Mario. At a hockey game very early in my life, I am sitting along the boards. The referee calls a faceoff an arm's length away, and in the split-second before the puck is dropped I sense that it's coming right at me. I duck and the puck slams into the back of my seat. Before I can react, the man in the row behind snatches the puck for his son.

Call it inner vision, a northern sense. The great ones anticipate time itself. Sometimes they appear to be doing many things at once, in the hurry of a video on fast-forward, so that they can act when called upon. It's a part of them, an organ, breath itself, a secret gift—stealth, quickness, intuition. Revealed in nothing more than a feint, a tilt of the skate blade.

The spectator remains in awe as a skeptical disciple disbelieves a miracle. But like the disciple, they will return for the prospect, the hope, of seeing it again.

Mug's real name was Douglas Minster Grunwald, but everybody called him Mug. We were both fifteen years old the day we got together, when he dropped his newspaper bag at the side of the rink, laced up skates he had brought along, and played ice hockey against the neighborhood kids. The Saturday we met the Grunwald's telephone rang into the night because dozens of subscribers had not received their newspaper, had missed their Ann Landers and the daily crossword puzzle.

We played against eight ten-year-old boys from the neighborhood. The Scrambled Eights we called them. And on the sidelines for reasons that were never clear was Brandy, a neighbor's St. Bernard. Before each game against the Scrambled Eights, Mug and I would stand at center ice and sing a song of our choosing—the theme from *The Beverly Hillbillies*, or "Mares Eat Oats and Does Eat Oats," or do mouth sounds that simulated the instruments to the theme song of the movie *Shaft*. Mug and I were like clumsy ravens badgered by sparrows, dodging, weaving, going nowhere, losing ground. Win or lose, we left the ice in triumph.

At other times, on nights after my father had flooded the rink, Mug and I played under a single naked lightbulb. I wore a battered fedora of Father's and skated in and out of shadows on the smooth ice. My own shadow loomed over the plywood boards we shot pucks at, rose into the night sky.

One day when we were alone on the ice, Brandy went berserk and suddenly lunged at Mug and held him in his teeth, dragging my friend by his arm across the rink. The beast, who until that moment had been calm at the rink's edge, ripped a hole in Mug's coat and shook him in his jaws like a rag doll, whipping up ice and snow. I struggled with the flank, and fistfuls of fur came off in my hands as I cried bitterly, sure my friend would be badly hurt.

Brandy was getting a better hold of Mug, closer to his throat, when behind me I heard the back door slam and saw Mum, wide-eyed and crazed, like a woman possessed. Brandy, too, looked up at the sound, and then, to Mum's screams and exaggerated shooing motions of her arms, the dog dropped Mug to the ice and wandered off, looking bored.

Mug was struggling to his feet as I rushed to him. "Had no idea Brandy wanted the Zamboni driver's job," Mug said, brushing his jeans of snow, his mocking smile returning. "We would have accommodated him, don't you think?"

"That was a bad one," I said later, shouldering his papers as we made our way down the lane. The dog's saliva was smeared over Mug's collar to a gaping hole down the back of his coat. Mug's hands shook as he pushed hair out of his eyes.

I said I was sorry I didn't do more to help him. I'd read that to stop an attack dog you were to hit hard the top of his head. But in the crisis I'd not been able to think straight. "I don't know, I've never felt so rattled. Brandy could've really hurt you."

Perhaps it was the way I trembled as I spoke, but Mug hugged me hard, for a long time wouldn't let me go. We walked through the snow arm in arm not saying a word. Not since my grandfather died had I felt so close to someone. A month earlier Father had taken a picture of me at Christmas, with a tape recorder at my side. I'd use the recorder to produce mock radio dramas and practice my technique as a news interviewer. The tape recorder was something I'd asked for, thought that I truly wanted. But there was no elation in my face as I posed before Father for the official holiday picture. It was Christmas Day and my thin face was pale, lips blood-red, while my arms splayed like willow branches on my bedspread. I sensed that Mug saw me as I did, a skinny nervous boy cracking under the strain of being completely different, of having no one to talk to. In a queer stupor that summer I had stuck my hand through the screen of a whirling fan, cut my fingers so badly that they had to be bandaged. Mug didn't know that one Saturday morning at breakfast, while Father asked me to pass the butter for his toast, I'd blacked out and slipped to the floor under the kitchen table, where I shook for more than a beat before I came to. Take him to the doctor? Nah, Father said. The boy's nervous, that's all. Growing pains.

When quiet is the institutionalized terror, rebellion is wasted. If there are no words, where is the growth? I am nine years old standing before a patch of deep water, a foot or two over my head, about a distance of six, maybe seven feet. One by one other boys in my swim class had swum across, slapping the water like disabled seahorses. They all had passed me by, jumped ahead, did their first swim, then squealed as they reached the other side. The patch of water was no longer than the size of an average man, but longer now as I think of it than the widest ocean. I would not budge. One counselor looked at me in disgust, another gave me a little push. "C'mon! C'mon!" my classmates and friends jeered from the other side. But for the life of me I couldn't move. Finally, I gathered my towel, and without saying a word or shedding a tear, got on my bike and rode home.

Walking arm in arm with my new friend, I told myself that my family's myth was based on a lie. I had not been touched by God with some inner strength to endure. In Keppel, you were guided by an inner moral compass to hold back the deepest pains, the sharpest sorrows. Even a desperate need to talk was a Keppel taboo, but it was one I found I had to break. I had never felt so scared and lonely.

"You know, Mug, I gotta tell you," I said, gripping him at the elbow. "My father . . . Well, it's about his family, I don't know . . ."

Mug was head and shoulders taller than me and he looked down into my eyes.

"I don't know, there's just nothing," I said, muttering into his shoulder. "No pictures. No visits. I know there's this girl cousin, so he's gotta have either a brother or a sister. But I'll bet they're just orphans who've gone different ways." I told him about the cedar chest, about the picture of the little girl, the clippings, how the key ring had suddenly disappeared.

Mug bent down and snatched a handful of snow. In spring we'd strip ladyfingers of frozen maple sap from overhanging branches and eat them with cool grains of spring snow. In winter we ate the fluffy stuff.

He handed me a bit of snow and it felt nice on my tongue. I wondered if I had said too much as Mug suddenly pulled his hand away.

Then he was gone, all arms and legs, leaping over a snowbank and into a clear drift, flapping to make the perfect angel. Mug, the clown, nothing is ever as it seems. A joke. Take no offense, it is just his way.

"Well, if you're a son of an orphan, then I'm an orphan shot through and through," he said as he rushed up to me. "I've the Viking blood, my friend!" And then he rose up and bayed at the sky. Like a madman. Mug was tall and lean, with straight blond hair and broad shoulders for his age; his parents were squat Scottish and Irish working class who followed closely the laws of a reformed Protestant church. His father was a cop whom Mug didn't see much of and his mother, who people called Mother Hubbard, took in more foster children than anyone else in town and was always taking care of a little kid that Mug didn't know. Once, I'd seen Mug trip and knock down a foster brother, whose head cracked against a concrete floor. "It's all right. He has the hardest head," he said. Mug bayed again. A stray dog stopped and looked at him. Mug's angel in the snow was a thing of beauty, larger than life, so out of touch with reality that no matter what your hurt inside all you could do was smile and laugh.

"Did you know I started this thing," he said, pulling the bag of papers from my shoulder and transferring it to his, "because I'd gotten into 'Today's Child'—you know, the column that matches lonely little fuckers with foster parents. I've been looking in old back issues for my picture for months. I've not found it yet . . . but, hey, why don't you join me? We could look for your dad."

That winter I went with my friend and scoured the musty-smelling newspaper supply rooms near the loading dock of the

Keppel Advance, looking for clues. Year after year of papers were piled up there. I found the front-page story of Bruce Grantham, a first cousin on Mum's side, a junior hockey star and straight-A student, who died tragically, falling to his death while working on a freighter on the Great Lakes. There was Great Uncle Reuben, Grandfather's brother, who earned an obit with a photo for working up the ranks at the waterworks. He made chief foreman, the highest position he could obtain without a high-school diploma, when the first pollution plant was built. It's now called the Reuben T. Grantham Sewage Treatment Plant. There was my birth notice: short and sweet, a twenty-word ad, Mug noted, the base rate. Just as I figured, my father's parents weren't printed in the notice, but Mug said that was common enough, that everybody in town knew where people came from so why pay the extra?

Sure enough, there was no birth notice around the day Douglas Minster Grunwald was said to be born. And as far as we could learn, little Mug never appeared as the featured orphan in "Today's Child." "I knew it! I knew it!" Mug cried, overjoyed, sitting cross-legged in the paper's supply room. "I'm not one of them! I'm not one of anyone's!" Months later Mug would leave Keppel, go north with the man who had taken a job as a district police chief. My dear angry friend was free to believe he was descended from Norse kings, to be as reckless and alone as a wild horse.

The first snowflakes in Antarctica, those that today are compressed beneath miles of ice and snow, could have fallen off the backs of mammoths or blown from the broadleaf trees that once grew there.

Antarctica used to be in a temperate zone where ice and snow did not stay year-round. But when the weather changed and temperatures remained cold, glaciers formed, locking under them green hills, valleys of seasonal landscapes.

Antarctic icebergs are not like the ones that resemble mountains and sink revealing only the tips—one-eighth of their size and one-tenth of the weight. Antarctic bergs are much larger and more likely to look like masses of white hills and flat plains. Some can be several miles across, weigh billions of tons. If the largest iceberg could be delivered intact to New York Harbor, it could provide enough fresh water to meet the drinking and washing needs of New Yorkers for fifty years.

Industrial designers have been working on elaborate plans—such as spraying an iceberg with an insulation compound similar to that used in home construction, covering it with a dark-colored tarp to reduce melt, and rigging it with high-powered motors—to transport icebergs to desert lands like Saudi Arabia and Southern California. The Saudis have spent small fortunes on harnessing icebergs for fresh water, and although a plan that makes economic sense has yet to be devised, the dream lives on. One day, Saudi princes promise, Arabs will be drinking water that was once snow falling on the backs of prehistoric beasts.

My brother Jim had a way on ice. Straight lines and deception. A heron at dawn. At the earliest age, Jim, the hockey player, could size up others: assess their ability to turn, to stop, dissect their center of gravity. He skated off players learning speed, crowded those with reach, poke-checked others. Then he would take over, exerting himself only as much as necessary to get the puck and hold on to it. Occasionally, he would throw it my way for a give and go, but usually he'd leave me be, do it alone.

Jim was discovered by Bill Fleming, a former pro with the Hershey Bears and coach of The North Stars, eight- and nine-year-olds who played the best teams from Derby, Gideon, and Sullivan Shores. The first time I saw Bill Fleming he was entering Phyllis's Beauty Shoppe, the only place in town where hair stylists worked. Phyllis's had been bought out by Jenkins Funeral Home, and old man Jenkins had put the stylists to work on the hair of corpses after hours and on weekends. Since then, business had gone bad, and I wondered, looking at the big man opening the ground-glass door of the beauty shop, if he knew that his hair stylist did corpses in off-hours. I went home trying to imagine a former Hershey Bear under a white cone, reading a women's magazine in an empty salon.

But Father had nothing but respect for Bill Fleming. No one else in Keppel had quit school to fight in the Korean War (even lied about his age so he could serve), Father said. He never actually played for the Hershey Bears, but he had a respectable tryout, more than anyone else in town could say. He had married Marge Saunders, the best-looking girl in town, had two blond twins, Rick and Ron, and started Fleming Cartage, a moving company. That would have been enough to earn him the respect of everybody in Keppel, but with the 1948–49 Grey Devils, the Junior B hockey squad, he broke all scoring records and led the team to its first and only provincial championship. My father said the orange and gray banner that hung in the rafters of the arena was there thanks to Bill Fleming.

At Jim's tryouts I stood beside my father at the open end of the arena while my mother and other parents and children sat huddled beneath aerial heaters in the grandstands. Father wore his dress Hudson's Bay jacket, the bright red one with a wide black stripe across the middle, and kept his arms crossed high in his chest, like a ship's captain studying the sea. The crispness of my brother's passes and the snap of his shots came partly from our practicing on the rink, and I said so, but soon Father scolded me: "Shhhh! Go to your mother if you want to yak."

Across the ice and behind the players' bench, Bill Fleming looked on. His hands were always behind his back, out of sight. Everything appeared too tight, too precise, like the men in *Rex Morgan, M.D.* Looking back, I wonder if this distinctiveness wasn't in the cut of his clothes—the exactness of the expensive and carefully tailored garments in a town of loose-fitting coats and off-the-rack suits. Beneath his hat's natty brim, Fleming's blue eyes, buried under salt and pepper eyebrows, never strayed from the surface of the ice. Once, he glanced and waved an index finger in Father's direction and in reply Father broke into a smile as broad as I'd ever seen, then jerked a nod Fleming's way.

After a newspaper article appeared about Jim, calling him a promising newcomer, my brother's hockey became everything to Father. He clipped nutrition articles from *Reader's Digest*, bought the unabridged rulebook for minor hockey, and blended high-octane milkshakes to beef Jim up. "Do you think I should call Bill about that new interpretation about interference?" he'd ask Mum, or "I'm sure that tryout from Gideon is using an illegal stick—Should I call Bill on it?" When Father tucked in Jim at night in the bed next to mine, he'd tell him that to get to sleep he should imagine himself doing back crossovers on a gigantic figure eight so that—even when he was sleeping—he'd be building his skating skills. "Good night, boy," he'd say to me, "sleep well," which in itself was amazing. Until Jim began trying out for Bill Fleming's hockey team, I don't remember Father ever coming to our room at night.

Most employers gave the town's former hockey warriors a couple of days off to "train" when the Old Timers Game came around each year. (Mostly they yakked about the old days, drinking gin in the back room of Fred's Barber Parlor.) A tilt between former hockey players from the Grey Devils and aging ex-pros of the Maple Leafs, the game rivaled the Christmas tree burning as the most popular wintertime event. Fans stocked up on envelopes and pencils at Bentley Office Equipment because Shift-Key Morrison, a store clerk and former Grey Devil center, received the most time off—a week with pay. Players employed as drivers and warehouse workers at Brewers' Retail worked only half-days for a week, and for two days Fleming shut down the cartage business. The newspaper's grocery-ad edition did spot-color profiles for a month of Wednesdays, stories on such greats as Max Bentley, Teeter Kennedy, and Turk Broda. Tickets were hard to come by the year Jim made the team, but Fleming, the pride of the Grey Devils old-timers squad, had put two aside for Jim and my dad.

I knew something was wrong that night after the game when Jim and Dad were silent during the television commercials. In our house, we talked only during the ads, and after the first sequence of them had come and gone, I began to wonder. "So, how was it?" I asked, during a particularly dull Geritol spot. But Father only shook his head. I could see Jim was crying and when I approached him he ran out of the room.

All the kids were talking about it the next day at school. Bill Fleming had the puck. First he'd beaten Hall of Famer Bob Pulford along the boards. Then he'd slipped it through the legs of Allan Stanley, the defensive specialist. Shift-Key was camped at the side of goalie Turk Broda. He had to get the puck there, elude the checking of Larry Hillman. Bill Fleming reared to the right, then went up on one leg, an inch or so off the ice. The puck lay at his feet but no one moved toward it. Broda rose out of his crouch; Stanley stopped at the right circle. Everyone was watching as Bill Fleming lifted to his full height, his forward movement keeping him suspended there, like a walrus harpooned, before he came crashing down onto his back on the ice. Before the St. John's Ambulance crew could get there with its gurney, before the team's trainer in new sneakers and towel swinging at his waist, before Marge Saunders had screamed her first scream, thousands of people filled to the rafters of Keppel Arena knew that Bill Fleming was dead.

That night I sat in strange silence with my father as he listened to television comedians, their wisecracks about wives, the digs at mothers-in-law. "Is there anything you can tell me?" I asked. "No, boy," Father said at length. "Just go upstairs." Father liked the jokes men in suits told about wives and cars. He didn't laugh but he would smile until his cheekbones pressed his eyes shut and made them disappear. The furrows of his brow vanished and his round full face looked smooth and clear, like a doll's. In a moment the joy would vanish. Deep lines in his forehead, thickening eyebrows, and dark eyes would return, and before long, before the trick dogs, the standup comics, the crooners and the man who kept a dozen plates spinning on a church-basement table, my father would be asleep.

While trying to sleep that night, I watched as shadows from the leaves of an elm tree danced on the wall of our room. I'd been waiting my whole life for something to happen. Now that something had, I felt nothing, only deadening silence, the pressure of another long, lonely night, while my parents were downstairs before the blaring set, looking on, mute, forever mute. I wanted to scream, tear at my hair, my flesh, gouge my eyes. Instead, unable to do as my brother had done, to imagine endless back crossovers on a gigantic figure eight, I stayed awake until dawn, listening to deep breathing, the athlete's sound sleep.

"Here I am," Father said that morning as he threw open the back door, his arms outstretched, holding a goalstick. "Mister Zero— The Shutout King." In his buckled-down galoshes, he inched slowly onto the slick ice of the rink. Using the stick to support himself, the sturdy round man crept along to the goalmouth of the hockey net. Here he sprinkled snow to steady his footing on the ice and then he hunched over, leaning on the goalstick. Behind him not a sliver of daylight escaped. There wasn't a space big enough to get a pea, let alone a puck, past him. "Just try to score," he said.

Jim and I peppered shot after shot at him and he blocked them all. "Mister Zero," he cried, laughing. "You just can't score." Soft rubber pucks buried in his flannel jacket, rebounded hard off his knees, slammed into his goalstick. We swarmed around him, tried give-and-goes, slapshots, snapshots, onetimers. But Father was unbeatable. "Mister Zero," he shouted again and again. "You just can't score."

After several minutes, Jim bore down hard on the wing, feinted to the left, and backhanded a shot across my father's body. Beaten, Mister Zero looked behind him, but the puck had not gotten through. It had somehow lodged in the crook between his elbow and chest. "You're back, kid," my father cried as my brother bounded into the house to shed his jacket, put on his team sweater. "You're back on top."

When we were alone Father shuffled aside, offering me half the net to shoot at. "C'mon boy, give me your darnedest. The first goal against Mister Zero. Soon to be Mister One . . . Take your best shot. Break the spell."

The puck was lying at center ice. When playing with goalies, Jim and I used soft-rubber pucks, but when they were struck just so, at the heel of the stick on the downward arc of a slapshot, they could really fly. I swung with all my might and before my father could move the puck struck him in the stomach and he went down in a heap. He writhed, his face contorting in pain. Ice chips clung to his thick jacket, speckled the sole of his galoshes. I hurried toward him, but secretly I had wanted to do what I had done.

His black eyes flashing, Father rose to face me. "YOU!" he cried. But I stood still, rooted in place. I would not back off. His lips trembled with something more he wanted to say. But neither of us spoke. For as long as I stared ahead, his arm shook with the heavy blade of the goalstick poised to strike.

s n o w

Toboggan rides. Caterpillars to butterflies of white spray. Legs wrap about hips, one upon another, until, at the end, at the curve of the wooden bell, the smallest pair sprouts overtop, dangling.

Speed, rushing wind, and stinging ice pellets excite riders into a silent frenzy, a strange stillness. The air nips. Sounds are muffled. Or caught in the throat unheard. Others spatter on the frozen ground like sharp pine needles from a tree.

The first day of The Big Snow I was lounging on the sofa, watching snow fall and *I Dream of Jeannie* when Father caught me at it. Helen was in her room; Jim was in the basement, building up his throwing arm by hurling a baseball into a pile of waste fiberglass insulation.

"Are you watching this program, or not?" my father said as he entered the room.

"Huh . . . I mean, pardon me?"

"The television. If you're not going to watch it, turn it off. If you're going to watch it, sit around straight and watch it!—TVs pull a lot of hydro," he said, staring at the set as Jeannie twirled and hopped into the arms of a U.S. astronaut. She was smiling at the American actor as Dad sat down into his La-Z-Boy chair.

"Eh? What's this show called, son?" Father had come in from trying to stay ahead of the storm by snowblowing what he could. White clouds flew from the curved chute of the snow machine as Father pressed forward toward the street. The chained tires churned through the deepest drifts. My father was a gladiator, holding high the black handles of the angry-sounding snow beast like the reins of a chariot. When he stopped, Mum met him at the back door and with a broom whacked him about the back, torso, and legs. Snow fluttered to the warm cement, melting. Ice bits hugged the moistened fibers at the upturned cuffs of his work pants.

"I Dream of Jeannie—Larry Hagman and Barbara Eden star. I don't know if it will do anything but it's got its moments. Hagman's an astronaut who finds a genie in a bottle after a splashdown. Still . . ."

"Uh huh." Jeannie was sprawling on cushions, pouting. "Well, it's almost over, eh? Get me a Coke, would you? Jeepers, is it snowing out there."

During The Big Snow, when even my father was obliged to abandon his traveling salesman's work because the roads and highways were closed, when for three days the snow kept falling and no one came in or out of Keppel, Father told me that what set me apart from my brother and sister was the way I watched television. I never let the TV get my full attention and instead observed whoever was in the living room with me, or gazed idly out the picture window in front. In my father's house, I lived in a constant state of anticipation, ready to spring into action if anything happened. I'd never encountered much of anything that deserved my full attention.

Father, on the other hand, was an early convert to TV. Nightly rituals began with three drumbeats: the slam of Father's car door, the slap of the screen door, and the clunk of the toilet seat against the tank as he pissed into the bowl. Mum was fixing the meal that was warming on the stove. Father and Mum would talk for a while and then he would turn on the television and watch.

"I don't get it, boy," Father said, after a long swig on his Coke. "The TV's on and there you go staring out the window. You know, there's work to be done if you don't want to watch. But if you're gonna watch, watch for pity's sake."

"Would you drop it, Dad. I'll help out later, you know that. Just let me be." After the rink incident, I had begun little by little to speak up for myself. Not take great strides, mind you, but I'd begun to feel that Father would stop short of hitting me.

Snow-blowing was a "one-man operation," as my father said, but every autumn he took me to a place in the bush to help him haul firewood for heating the house that winter. He had a deal with the landholder that in exchange for clearing a stand of trees of dead wood we'd get a season's supply of fuel. Father would straddle fallen trees with a secondhand chainsaw that roared like a jackhammer as I hurried behind him, picking up the logs he had cut and running them to be stacked in a clearing. "'You can't handle THIS, boy!" he yelled once when I'd asked to give the cutting machine a try. "Pick up the logs!" Father wore no safety glasses but rather closed his lips tightly and squinted to see where to cut. Woodchips and sawdust flew from the dead trees to his face and onto his unbuttoned lumberjack shirt and sweatshirt.

It was later that year, after our faceoff on the rink. Our custom had been that when the chainsaw ran out of fuel, I'd lug it back to our hired truck to gas it up, leave it there, and bring sandwiches to Father, who'd be resting in the woodlot. This day Father held the chainsaw stock-still with his forearm extended, and when I took it in two hands, the tool dropped like a stone, narrowly missing my feet. "Every year," he sighed. "When are you gonna put some meat on your bones, son? Here, I'll give you a hand." But suddenly, I yanked the chainsaw from him. "Not this time, you won't," I said, trembling in anger. Buckled under the weight of the chainsaw, I turned and walked to the truck. For once, I didn't feel his eye boring hard into my back, unnerving me. Fuck him, I thought. Let him take Jim next time; I'd have nothing more to do with him.

Mad as hell and swinging the bag of sandwiches, I made my way back to my father. But when I got there he was sitting on a log in the woods, his arms heavy between his legs like a veteran hockey player in double overtime. Even after I'd put the roast beef sandwich at his side, he didn't look up. Snow began to fall. When I took the first bite of roast beef, we both knew. I'd learned too well from my father how to shut down and fight off, how to keep what matters inside. There'd be no more talk. Maybe I'd never know anything about Father. But I knew one thing: The family was not big enough for me and him. Like Grandfather, I thought, I too would be driven out of Keppel.

We worked for hours as the snow fell, and when we were finished, we drove home with the back seat and truck box loaded to the axles with wood. The chainsaw—warm from my father's hands, the heat of the motor—we kept on the seat, in front, between us.

It was common that first-born sons in the north were called such names as Liquid Dog Shit (Itiktarniq) or Little No-Good Penis (Usukitat). When the boy called Liquid Dog Shit had grown old enough to understand the meaning of the name, Eskimo men poked him in the butt, crawled around on all fours, howled at the stars. Men frolicked about Little No-Good Penis like castrated clowns, made obscene gestures with their hands.

But both Liquid Dog Shit and Little No-Good Penis made roly-poly pantomime to silence the fat men. Or pranced in girly nonchalance to mark a man's bad marriage or his inability in the hunt.

If names alone defeat you, you can't be worth much.

After a dinner of whole milk, boiled potatoes, succotash, pot roast, and Jell-O on the first night of The Big Snow, we gathered in front of the TV. First up was *Bowling for Dollars*. Mum liked to watch the show partly because a bowling buddy, Millie Sturbridge, spent every Monday for years filling out postcards, and contestant bowlers often picked her card from a tumbling bin and shared fifty-fifty their winnings with her. Later, Mum would tell me that Millie had a huge crush on Bud Rangel, the host. After a few years of sending the postcards, she started attaching obscene stickers to them. Periodically, Bud would select one of them and, shaking his head, put it back into the bin, telling the television audience that the sender had forgotten to put down a phone number or the postal code that was required.

Although Mum never mailed a postcard herself, she liked the idea of it. "Wouldn't take much," she'd say. "Just scribble a little note . . . But I don't know, I can't seem to get around to doing anything about it." Mum was a crack five-pin bowler, regularly won the best woman's average in Keppel's ladies league. I urged her on, told her to telephone Bud Rangel personally and become a contestant bowler. But she demurred: "Not me, son. I couldn't take the pressure. I'd throw three gutter balls and that would be that."

With *Concentration*, Father demanded quiet as he mouthed the clues that would come into view. Mum held back, winking at me that she had already solved the riddle but never letting on when he came up with it. Mum watched TV not so that she could realize her dreams or make something better of herself, but so she'd have material to talk to Father about. She never swung a golf club in her life but knew about two-stroke penalties, double bogies, playing the ball where it lies. She memorized the sexist jokes and racist slurs told by American comics, so she could recount it all to my father late at night, under cover.

The first night of The Big Snow I had a nightmare. I was in a dark place, a coffin, I don't know, but I was alive and being touched by an old man, Grandfather, I thought, but I couldn't be sure. The bottles, the old man said, I'll bring the bottles up for you. I woke in a sweat and threw off my covers. Jim was sleeping soundly, as usual, and I tiptoed to the doorway of my parents' bedroom.

"Mum, are you awake?" I asked. Without hesitating, she sat up in the bed, almost as if she were expecting me. Perhaps she, too, had been lying awake.

"What is it, son? It's very late." I started to say something, then stopped, couldn't look at her in the shadows. If Mum were alone she would hug me, I thought, begin to talk to me in a way that mattered. In no time, the sun would be up and we'd be at the kitchen table, have gone through it all: the cedar chest, my fear and loathing of Father, the mystery of him. The burdens of this place, my life, would slowly lift.

Father moved in his sleep. I wished my father were not just absent but gone forever. Not dead, exactly, but gone all the same.

"Go back to bed," Mum said finally. "You'll feel better in the morning."

When I got back to my room, I stepped across to the window. Rime and hoarfrost are not snow but yet another type of ice crystal, ice cloud or water cloud. White, powderlike water vapor is frozen in air, trapped in the wind that meets the glass. I pressed my palm to the cold until the warmth left a handprint of clear glass to look through. Snow had blown in tight to the glass, so I could not see the street, the arc of the streetlamp, or the big flakes fluttering down. When it really stormed in Keppel, snow came down, not in a violent way, not like the anger of some god, but gently, continuously, until everything of any use was covered over and nullified. After a big snow in Keppel, there was no escape.

Scientists measure snow, label the crystals by such names as plate, stellar, and spatial dendrite. In cold laboratories, where temperatures are kept below zero and snow is examined under chilled slides, scientists have learned that snow forms from dust particles or minute crystals of sea salt; that it's a myth that no two snowflakes are alike; that near the freezing point snowflakes have been measured several centimeters across in calm air. That at the pole, crystals are like shot, as hard as nails.

But snow is to Eskimos what water is to pond life. Eskimos know if snow is compacted enough for a fifty-mile-per-day pace with dog teams to their hunting grounds; they know if snow cover on sea ice is safe or likely to dissolve into roiling water; they can follow even the faintest tracks. The best snow for igloo building is light to handle yet compacted, giving near-perfect insulation, making an igloo so strong that when finished a man the size of Bobby Hull can jump up and down on its dome and it won't collapse. Such snow can be cut and shaped more easily than any other building material known to man. Eskimos have lived for generations in the north because they know snow. In their language they have more than one hundred words for it.

"What the sam hill! When is it going to stop?" Father shouted. Mum murmured something I couldn't hear. It was daybreak. "I've just GOT to get out there; he depends on me," he said. A pause,

Mum's voice. "Oh whadda YOU know?" The door shut with a bang. He was gone. Jim sat bolt upright in bed and in a single breath began crying as if his heart would break. Mum arrived at his side, soundlessly, and looked at me while she patted Jim on the back. She looked drawn and worried, then nodded slowly and said, "Frank's." And I knew.

Frank's was Dad's best account, his first one in the western district, the largest but poorest territory in the local office of the Hudson's Bay Company. Frank Sherwood, a black sheep of a distinguished Toronto family, had opened a little corner store in the village of Kincardine the same day Dad inherited the west, and for some reason the merchant favored Father. There were many traveling salesmen from whom to choose, but Frank gave Dad his account, told him to hold on to the district because big business was coming.

A year later, true to Frank's word, the government announced the building of the Bruce Nuclear Power Development, a few miles from Kincardine, and the BNPD, as it became known, grew to become the largest nuclear power station ever built. Thousands of workers from Toronto came north, and Frank's corner Stop 'N' Shop expanded into Frank's Atomic SuperSaver, the largest supermarket around. At its peak, in one six-week summer period, Frank's sold more ground beef and summer sausage than any single independent supermarket in Canada (including Toronto); and in winter, no store did its business in pot roasts and hams. Once, the *Toronto Star* ran a personality profile on Frank, and though in the article he didn't say that he owed his success to his most reliable salesman, it seemed to me implied in every line. ("What is more important than anything else is having good people behind you. . . . In the country, folks are decent and respectful, don't bull—— them and they won't cross you, just treat 'em fair and square.") Pictured in the photo spread were citations from Red Meat for Real People and Food Relief for Biafra charities, and snaps of Frank with prime ministers—at the Dief for Beef dinner, and holding a pigskin in a close-up with Robert Stanfield. In a copy of the article Frank sent to Father, the millionaire grocer wrote along the border, "To my favorite salesman," and signed his name, "Frank."

Some said success had changed Frank when he began bypassing jobbers and middlemen, making deals directly with suppliers. But with my father there were no shenanigans. The stencil Frank used for his original paper bags (from dime to double-ply) was an exclusive of Dad's supplier, a small printing house not far from Keppel that had come to do nothing but Frank's bags for the supermarket. As a favor to my father and as a public symbol of his old-fashioned values, Frank didn't switch to plastic bags as the grocery chains were doing.

But such loyalty came at a price. The print shop did not have the capacity to do any more than two days' supply of paper bags on any given day, and because it was family run, they never put on a weekend shift. So once a week, Frank would always be low on stock. Dad routinely loaded bags into his green company car from stem to stern at dawn Tuesday, so he could personally deliver enough bags by opening time to tide them over. Only once, during the Christmas holidays, Frank was caught short and had to go to the IGA across town and pay premium for theirs.

So Tuesday mornings were everything to Father. After he dropped off the load of bags, he and Frank would take time out for coffee in the stockroom. Tuesdays weren't complete without his visit, he once told Dad. Sipping coffee from a quality paper cup, never Styrofoam, Frank would say he needed the connection with his past that Dad's visits gave him. He promised to never let my father down. He would keep saying no to the plastics salesmen from Downsview who batted his door like moths at a light.

Mum calmed Jim back to sleep, then touched the top of my head. She turned to me and smiled, mussed my hair, said that I was thinking too hard, that I was too much like her. "Don't be a worrywart, not like your mother," she said.

"I'm not, not really. I just want to know . . ."

"I know you do, son," she said as she leaned down and kissed me on the cheek. She had been crying, and even now tears were coming to her eyes. At a loss for words, I reached out and pulled her close.

"And don't be too hard on your father," she said at last as she turned to go. "He's a good man."

"Of course he is," I said.

"I love you so much," she said, her voice breaking as she walked away. "Remember that. But don't you worry about your father. He loves you in his own way. As you get older, you'll see."

An Eskimo woman stopped when she could no longer see the footprints of her mukluks in the snow. She put her back to the wind and squatted. With her baby covered under layers of animal skin on her back, she barely stirred.

The woman lost track of time. Occasionally she felt cold and stood up, shuffled her feet, walked with the wind at her back. Then she resumed her position on her haunches.

If the baby were to piss the clothes would have frozen stiff and soon they both would have perished. But the woman somehow knew when the baby had to go. In the only sudden movement she made, the woman swung the naked infant into the cold, shielding her baby against the wind. The baby pissed and then was placed back under the skins. He cried until he felt warm again, then suckled at her breast.

After three days and nights of this the storm finally ceased. Then the woman walked on.

Father slammed the door so hard the house shook and shreds of Corn Flakes and milk splashed from our spoons. Jim, Helen, and I had just sat down to breakfast. On the radio open line, callers were saying the shacks in Mudtown on the other side of the tracks were inundated, neighborhood dogs had gone missing, the storm had become a "doozie."

"Don't talk to me," Father hissed at Mum somewhere between the back door and the kitchen. "I could have made it, it wasn't so bad. . . . They're GOOFS, those cops!" he screamed. He hadn't gotten far. At the top of the Creamery Hill, he'd been turned back by police: all roads leading out of Keppel had been closed indefinitely due to heavy snow. Father was stuck at home until at least the following morning, police had said.

Father filled the space of our narrow hall. Our eyes met and held. I was afraid but wouldn't budge. At least something was happening, and I was damned if I were going to miss it. Snow covered him from his toes to the tip of his fine fedora. His hands were plunged in the deep pockets of his dress red-and-black Hudson's Bay coat. Dark wisps of hair fell down his face, one strand arced near his eye.

In such a mood, Father seemed capable of anything. But until this moment, the ferocity, the murderous potential, always had been withheld, bottled up, like some liquid high explosive in *The Avengers* or *Mission Impossible*. Like one of those bombs, my father rarely blew. Once, at the company warehouse, he'd thrown a carton of cigarettes at the head of a smart alec worker—a man six inches taller and fifty pounds heavier than he. The man had ducked, so the box missed. But the man hadn't retaliated. The quality of the savage in Father must have scared his foe off, made him feel that Father was capable of fighting back even as he received heavy blows, until there was no life left in him.

The truth was I wanted him to hurt me. To bellow "Jesus Christ!" and in three giant steps be upon me. I'd squirm so he couldn't get a firm grip on me, and with his thumb and forefinger he'd lift me from the chair as Mum tugged on his sleeve. Cereal, bowl, milk, the kitchen chair and all, would go flying. "It's not worth it, boy! BACK OFF!" he'd cry, then fling me aside like a sack of clothes. Gary Gilmore, executed for murder in America, never felt more alive than when he was getting brutally beaten by his own father. If he could live through that then nothing could touch him. This time I wouldn't look up, though I'd feel the pressure of him, hovering over me. Then Father would be gone, leaving me sprawled on the kitchen floor. "BOOM!" the door would slam. But instead there was only the sound of the door. Once again, my father had vanished. Blinded by tears, I too was gone, running free of Mum, leaving Jim and Helen muttering in their bowls.

Mum came to the door of my room, but I yelled, "NO!" I wouldn't talk. Anger was so much a part of my father's life, and even that I was shut out of. Say what you like about Gary Gilmore, but something happened to him—and people around him. Nothing, it seemed to me, would ever be expressed in my father's house. So I would follow that lead and do it one better. The silent treatment all around. The violence of silence is unspeakable, I thought, grinning for the first time that day. Don't speak when spoken to. The middle-class child's revenge. Lying in bed, staring at the ceiling, I thought how much Kurtz in *Heart of Darkness* made me think of my father. I gave Kurtz the murderous paternal gaze, assigned the mystery of Conrad's character to him. A difficult childhood, an old resentment, was not enough to explain his anger. Only the worst kind of human experience, only horror could have made it possible. In those dark, fiery eyes he carried a terrible secret, and it was that secret that was driving me away.

Winter's landscape encircles, presses down with the weight of gurgling pack ice, driving northerners deeper within themselves. Indoors, northerners clasp hands or warm them under legs. Brood. People of the north in heated sanctuaries appear sad, sullen, at best, contemplative. A river deepening in ice.

In the city summer breezes lift beads of sweat from flesh; words flow like savanna grass. Children run in the gusher of a tampered hydrant; scissors of tiny legs cut the humid night air. The southern child leaps, cleansed in spray. Friends join him against a streetscape of brownstones, bungalows, skyscrapers.

The north has no such brawny power. In the snow, children come together on a steep hill aboard a toboggan, stacked one upon the other like slats on a washboard. Enclosed from the elements at infancy, the northern child grows isolated from the union of lip and limb. He unfolds, by comparison, alone. Bundled up, northerners feel only their own sweat, clammy and uncomfortable, beneath wool and nylon.

Interiors. We are about interiors.

The future, Mum urged, lay in fireworks. I don't know how Mum found the way that morning to tell my father the rumor about the shop that printed bags for Frank's Atomic Super Saver. But then I've often underestimated her. When Mum was nervous or threatened, she talked a blue streak—like a woman possessed. She stood up to a mad dog, to Father on disposable diapers; she would do the same when the family was threatened. Mum weighed disaster in practical, not personal, terms. Family to her was something that had to endure, that was to be presented freshly scrubbed and in clean clothes every Sunday. If Father was a pent-up atomic blast, Mum was a neutron bomb. She was a Bloodworth, born to sacrifice. Give up her own life but leave the family structure standing.

Father had sold family packs, burning schoolhouses, sparklers, and firecrackers for holiday weekends. The time was right to expand into fireworks displays themselves, she said. Father had done the summer fireworks supervisor course at the Keppel Fire Department and had assisted with a show at the Keppel pioneer do. Mum did the books, knew fireworks was a forty-percent markup item. Sale of a single pack, she'd say, was more profitable than two dozen grocery bags.

Mum had followed Father into the bedroom that day and made her pitch. The paper bag concession was doomed, she said. Let it go. Mr. Hyslop, the aging owner of the print shop, was negotiating to sell out to a developer from Baltimore, and new owners were set to close the plant and sell to Burger Barn. Mum had heard talk about it at the bakery outlet. Tomorrow, the *Keppel Advance* would run the story on front page.

"Let Frank rant and rave," she said. "Fireworks are better than bags."

It was *Concentration* time, the afternoon version, when Mum led Father to the living room. "Call Frank after the show," she said. Father looked stunned, like Dagwood Bumstead, hair askew, business suit rumpled. Outside, the storm had not let up. Inside, Hugh Downs and the contestants were barely visible, fading in and out, obscured by broadcast interference, or snow.

In Keppel snow falls like the fake stuff in Hollywood, on currents of collective sighs, steadily, passionless. When you stare into it you can be hypnotized, bring on visions. Try to find its center, for the place of order, for the place out of which you can plan your next move.

When the American programs grew unwatchable due to the interference and "nothing" was on Canadian TV, Father turned off the set and faced us. Except for the rattle of the refrigerator, the house was quiet, and I pressed my hands tightly into the folds of my pajamas. The falling of the snow, my father said, had reminded him of a story.

Once long ago my father lived on a farm. For months in the winter he lived in virtual isolation from the outside world, behind towering white walls of snow. Between the barn and their small house—a distance of no more than one hundred feet—they tied a rope to grab hold of because blizzards made it impossible to see. He came to know the paths on their land like Eskimos learned to pick their way across seemingly endless landscapes of snow and ice.

One day, in the middle of a particularly wicked blizzard, my father said he had to drive a car to a place.

"Why was it so important? Was it an emergency?" I asked.

"Not in so many words," he said. "Just listen. 'For all intents and purposes, we may as well be living sixty miles within the Arctic Circle.' That's what Don McClintock, our history teacher, used to tell us when the snow was as bad as it was on that weekend. Snow fell for days on end. Bicycle racks and the Keppel cenotaph vanished. Even a farmer died. The poor bloke was searching for a calf gone astray during the night. He stopped behind a tree out of the wind to rest, fell asleep, and was found frozen to death the next day."

"Did you know him, personally, Dad? Did you know the dead farmer?"

"Just pipe down and listen," he said, whirling around. His eyes were fiery, and Mum's look was cautionary, pleading.

He muttered something, paused a long time, picked his teeth with a toothpick he kept in his breast pocket. Finally, he resumed.

"I liked snow. Like most kids. On the way to school we'd run with our coats flapping about, made snow angels and tasted flakes on our tongues. We'd make snowballs until our fingers were good and numb.

"But this day, you have to understand, was unlike anything I had ever seen. The snow was so bad at times I couldn't see the hood ornament. It was piled like cliffs, drifted like the Sahara. Cars partly covered in snow on the roadside reminded me of animal droppings. Tires were caked in ice and snow, utterly useless.

"The radio said that seven people had died near Buffalo. In one case rescuers uncovered a vehicle in which a man had frozen to death, only to find, buried beneath it, another car, with a young couple inside. All of them were buried alive."

Father was sitting forward now. His dark eyes glistened in the light of a table lamp; his face was a jack-o'-lantern's—pagan and triumphant, fleeting.

"I kept the car within the two narrow tracks of snow that were packed down in the driving lane by cars which had gone before me, and slowed down to about twenty miles an hour. I saw this small truck driving up behind me in the drift that was once the passing lane. When the truck was level to my car it veered toward an opening of blowing snow that was not an opening at all but the ditch. It went crashing into the snow, and then down an embankment. My first impulse was to stop, but if I put on the brakes on the ice I would have lost control, too. So I kept on going."

Father took a long pull on his Coke. "I didn't panic. That was the thing. I'm a lot smarter today—in this kind of weather I keep a snow shovel in the trunk, an extra coat and boots. But I didn't have any of those things, was wearing street shoes on my feet and a thin leather jacket that didn't even cut the wind."

Then Father turned my way, his face smooth and strangely innocent. There was a tear in his eye.

"I just let it go. Everything. Became blind to the cars being covered over with snow in the ditch, the ones in slow motion in front. All I wanted to do was keep the car in those ruts. That's all. If I let myself think of anything else I was sure I would slide off the road, get buried up, and freeze to death."

His voice trailed off to the sound of the wind that had picked up outside.

Just before he turned the television set on again, Father said he made it to his destination only to find that the people he had planned to meet had been forced to turn back.

Sorry was my game. When we brought out the board games the others won at Hands Down and Mum at Concentration. But in my father's house I was the master of Sorry.

In Sorry, there are perfect moments. You turn over the 1-Card, then follow it a turn later with a 4-Backwards; or use the 12-Card and a long slide, eliminating men; or play a Sorry and replace an opponent. With a Sorry your move is often obvious, to attack the frontrunner. But to win consistently, you must keep your motives hidden, not attract any attention to yourself.

Father was asleep on the La-Z-Boy by the time we sat down to play. Maybe Mum sensed I was at a breaking point, knew I was desperate for something to happen, I don't know. But when Jim cried out for a game of Hands Down she said no; she told Helen that tomorrow was another day, we would play Yahtzee then. She kept the lid on Concentration and we played Sorry game after game.

I chose the yellow men, the quiet colors, the ones that seemed to attract the least attention, and moved slowly, methodically around the board. When I eliminated a player I did it with humility; my "Sorry" had a sincere, plaintive tone. Yet, within, I was remorseless, even cruel, calculating the next move. I masked cunning with naïveté; intelligence with meekness. I cut down my opponents in deft, natural strokes, disguising the glee I felt. When Mum closed the lid on the box, told me I was a little angel and sent us all up to bed, I had won game after game.

That night as the snow fell on Keppel, keeping people trapped in their homes in a way they had not felt since '65, The Night the Lights Went Out, I lay awake and replayed my paths to repeated board-game victories. I was master of Sorry in training for games of a different kind, the ones my father and I would one day play.

When I awoke on the third day of The Big Snow and came downstairs, my father was on the rink in the half-light. For a short time that morning the snow had stopped falling. It must have taken him hours, but Father had shoveled the surface of the rink and now was flooding the ice.

Before the others were awake, I ran upstairs to put on my clothes, returning to the back room for my coat, hat, and skates. But, outside, Father was nowhere to be seen.

Snow began falling again, like sugar this time, dry and coarse. I flung the puck onto the rink and it slapped the rink's hard ripples, slipped through center like a balloon, and disappeared over iced edges into the snow.

I skated around the sides of the rink, my hands clasped at my back, circling the center, leaving it untouched, and kept the blades on the ice down the straightaway, picking them up only in the corners. Here the scoring of the surface was deepest. Crossover steps and turn to straightaway. Crossover steps and turn to straightaway. My speed constant, I eased my weight down my spine to balance my hips and the top of my knees.

I heard a familiar sound and stopped, sending a shower of ice chips into the snowy air. The motor of Father's car rumbled and whined and then the car was gone, taking my father, now a fireworks salesman, toward the roads that were not yet clear.

Near the entrance to the rink Father had plunged a hockey stick into a snowbank, and it had shifted forward, marking a black hole like the one left by the puck I had yet to recover. When the snow started falling heavily again, I slowed to a stop, and in the swirling white, stared alternately at the two black holes in the snow.

light

The brown of Tim Horton's sucks me in. The crust of white bread, Bailey's Irish Cream. No, it's softer, plainer, unpolished. Like Canada itself. For years a friend who owns a paint factory has been selling a color blend that he calls Tim Horton Brown. Nothing sells better. Industrial clients buy it to cover bathroom walls and lunchrooms; retailers choose it for stockrooms, sales bunks.

Patrons of Tim's are sucked in, too. Horny Tim's, they call it. The morning crew, their cars idling on cushions of exhaust, snag complementary *Globes* and *Suns* and turn pages, cradling Tim Horton Brown cups of hot coffee. They speak from thawing lips of road conditions, last night's game, home repairs. Women in uniform once taught third grade, never married. Or they're married with a couple of kids. Who can afford three nowadays? They call folks "Hon" or "Dear." Outside, kids wave at their working moms, but inside they button up, barely speak as they snatch the steaming white dough of crullers they get for free.

A touched-up reproduction of an oil painting depicts the hockey player Tim Horton in the classic pose, stopping, slashing a mist of ice and snow. Every Saturday night Tim dropped to his knees as the shooter—Bobby, or Rod, or Gordie—drove the puck toward the net. Then Tim would headman the puck to Red Kelly to Dickie Duff to Davey Keon. In life, he played the power play, blocked the heavy, hard ones in shinguards and padded pants. In death, his speeding car spun out of control, crashed into concrete.

I had been in line at the Tim's in Windsor for so long I was beginning to think that I would be late for work. Three people stood between me and the counter girl. I'd arrived at 11:30 P.M. because the usual wait was fifteen minutes or so, and it took me about the same time to drive through the city streets and get to my copy desk at the *Star* for the midnight-to-eight shift, where I wrote headlines, fixed sentences, and corrected spelling for a living.

I was thirty-three. For seven years I'd taken newspaper jobs, but never so far away from home. I'd worked up to this: a sports column at a three-thousand-circ weekly, speed-writing obits of dead farmers and women's club leaders, Orange Day parades. Proceeds from Saturday night bingos and progressive euchre parties put money toward the Orange Hall, where for more than a century farmhands and insurance agents had been damning Poperism, grousing about the modern ways. "It'd be a different story if the Protestant preachers would get up and do a little more of the proper kind of talking," I'd put down in one interview. "Why, some of them are associating with Catholic girls, and one thing and another. You can't do anything about it."

The day I moved to Windsor, my father arrived at the appointed hour in his fireworks delivery van, we loaded it up with my belongings, and he drove with me down the highway. Father didn't stay long on these trips, never overnight. We got on with the job, like monks changing missions, packing up, saying little. We wrapped the dishes in the newspapers that I'd worked for, with the stories that carried my name, toted milk cartons of my records and books, lifted my desk into the van and then drove for miles down the highway. He chose the fastest route to my new home, unloaded in half the time it took to load, and with the suddenness of his arrival, Father was gone.

That night in Tim Horton's parking lot, women in tight leather jackets sprawled on motorcycle seats, oblivious to the cold, their breath mingling with engine exhaust. Bearded men in black leather jackets with thumb-size zippers stood in line. Footprints of slush clung to the floor like iron filings attracted to a magnet. The regulars, mere boys from auto assembly lines, shuffled about nervously, murmuring, not about their jobs, the layoffs recently announced, but about the erratic idling of their reconditioned rigs—Chevies, T-Birds, GTOs.

"Two double chocolate donuts, large coffee, black," I said, the words sounding strange in my mouth, like someone else's. I'd never felt part of life here. Windsor, the end of the line. I dated women from time to time, never for long. Mostly, I imagined myself a night creature crawling out from under a rock. I hadn't found what I wanted to do, was beginning to think that I'd never fit in, not here, not anywhere. If only I'd been able to get the job with the CBC in the far north out of college when I still believed my work could make a difference then everything would have been all right. Now I wasn't so sure.

"For here or to go, dear," the waitress said as she poured my coffee. "To go," I said. In a minute I'd slip into my car and drive on to work. I'd put my Tim Horton's bag on the seat beside me and steer through the streets.

Windsor neighborhoods were once working class, full of Eastern European immigrants who'd never married and who tinkered at metal salvage in garages, naked bulbs burning above them all night. In those days there were four cars to a household, three working, one on the mend. In recent years the surrounding houses had emptied, were gutted or condemned. The old workers were gone, their family line died out or laid off. No new jobs or families have emerged in their place.

I'd been working for three years in Windsor, the most southerly of cities. Canada's Sun Belt. Fifty-seven varieties. Where the tomatoes come from. One especially humid summer day, sitting at an outdoor cafe, I fainted and the servers laid me out over three black plastic chairs and revived me with ice. When I recovered I tipped the waiter, and went north, to Detroit, to see the Tigers, then strippers from Chicoutimi and Shawinigan at Jeremy's Bar.

In Jeremy's, women who called themselves Josie, Yvette, and Susie had trim, firm breasts and tiny tattoos on their shoulders, blew rabbit puffs and gyrated on wooden boxes for men with cash: baseball players, CBC managers, auto plant poobahs. Pariahs and ghosts, the dancers worked for a few years, then poof! they were gone. Once the United Way of Windsor turned down thousands of dollars in donations the dancers had collected for charity. In public life, these women didn't exist. Jeremy's doormen had it better. College men pocketed as much as a thousand dollars a night in bribes from tour guides escorting groups of Japanese and German auto executives to front-row tables and backroom rendezvous. Upon graduation, they went to Wall Street or scored a job with GM or Ford, never Chrysler.

When there wasn't a Red Wings or a Tigers game, no one was out. Fancy homes on Victoria Avenue were dimly lit. I'd pass a Woolworth's, Century 21. Midnight in Windsor was just like home.

Shut your eyes in the light of an arctic spring and your inner lids blaze florid and mauve. To sleep you'll need blindfolds, the kind Fifties starlets once wore as sleepwear, to block the light.

Track an arctic fox and against the snow they'll disappear, vanish as if brushed away. Hunters under the spell of a mirage imagine they are tracking polar bears, but they're not, merely ptarmigans. In the movie *White Dawn*, dying whalers catch sight of their Eskimo rescuers—fearful-looking men in stone goggles with thin slits. The goggles themselves are nothing but stone knobs tied with laces of animal skins. A narrow opening lets through just enough light in a northern spring so that you can see the outlines of objects on the snow.

Is that a small animal close by, or a large animal at a distance? Its outline blurs. For miles the landscape doesn't change, its color and texture uniform. Under the even, unshaded light, objects lose autonomy, coherence. The real and the imagined become one.

One day in Windsor a friend discovered he could not step from the landing of his apartment building to the stair below. "What is happening to me!" he yelled as he tried again and again to take another step. I put my arm around him, and we moved slowly down to the street. I drove him to a hospital's emergency room, and after a battery of tests, doctors declared that my friend's vision had suddenly and inexplicably become impaired: he had lost the ability to perceive depth. He now wears specially made glasses, even in the shower, so that he can move through the world without fear of falling.

Snowblindness is so terrible, so paralyzing, you cannot take a step.

The reporters never looked up from their work when the night editors came in. At first, I'd brought them the occasional cruller or cream-filled donut from Tim's but they'd showed no appreciation so I'd stopped doing that. Still, it must have been one of them that took the telephone note for me that night. The note itself was unsigned. It was tucked in the keyboard space bar of my computer, the one against the wall where I sat beside K, the ex-biker.

K was once a *Star* columnist but he got on the bad side of the newspaper's Roman Catholic management when he divulged the toe-sucking secrets about Father Pierce, a priest who liked young boys. K also researched allegations of corruption in the United Way, *Star* management's favorite charity. One day readers were turning to K's ombudsman column, "Action Line," and the next they were reading in K's former space sunglass-buying tips in a syndicated medical column from Burnaby. In a single stroke, K the writer had been wiped out. For the last seven years he had been the senior person on the night desk. No special announcement was ever made; most readers, I found out later, thought he had moved on to Toronto.

K's Tim Horton coffee stood open and cold. He was most likely in the can for a smoke. The instruction manual of the new computer system lay piled on scraps of papers, notebooks, old copies of the *Star*. K hadn't been taking many stories for editing and headlines lately. Instead, he was making an intensive study of our new computer software. K's plan was to rewrite passages of the master manual for pagination, the new page-production system the *Star* was introducing, then arrange with an out-of-province printing company to typeset the changes so that they would match the manual's typographic specifications. Only a few, select pages would be altered, then replaced in the manual. A foolproof plan of sabotage, K said, that could never be traced back to him. "The system won't crash," he said, a gleam in his eye. "Just get reamed out a little."

The note read: "YOUR FATHER CALLED. PLEASE RETURN ASAP." Amazing. Father never called. Never speak or write until spoken to or written to was our motto. Could it be there had been a death in the family? Why hadn't Mum called? No matter how many phone numbers I had accumulated through my life, Father's was the line leader, reporting in my mind like a Detroit River gunshot. Over the years I'd picked up the phone hundreds of times and started to punch it in, but then think better of it and choose a second number, a chum's, an old girlfriend's. These days I often got K's answering machine, his guttural mutterings. ("I'm out; far out. Leave a message.") Or K himself, saying he had to scram before he went crazy and trashed a day editor. He'd rant about selling his house, moving to Vancouver, La-La Land, or worse still, Calgary.

I didn't travel much but I liked to run. Once, I ran alone for miles in the bitter cold. Footfalls hit squarely on hard-packed snow, crunching; hips, as if on a tight hinge. Eyelashes moist with Vaseline; a tuque to my brow. I recalled Father's story of the drive in the snowstorm, but instead of fear, I gave myself away to wonder. I scaled small hills of dazzling brilliance, what the Eskimos call *quamaneq*, the shaman light. *Quamaneq* is a fireball, a burning bush. In the darkest night, shamen see all: a single hair on a newborn's head, an owl in a snowstorm. Dogs and wolves exchanged howls. My yellow scarf was tied tightly around my waist, my chest covered in nylon and wool, extended. For hours, I ran.

A German shepherd—at first I thought it was a wolf, its howl was so haunting—leaped into the road and raced toward me. I turned and the dog's head filled my view, its nose clipping snow. It chose the best attack angle and came even faster. He was about to pounce when a shrill whistle split the air. Then he was gone.

Exhausted and thrilled, I paused at my door. Here in the blowing snow I imagined the red-faced warrior, Windigo, the Algonquin spirit of the wild. Hockey scores, much to my astonishment, were meaningless.

For a year between my second and third years at college I took a job at a mall in Galt, a town of industrial plants and convenience stores, for the experience on the microphone, to boost my confidence as a future broadcaster to Eskimos. At first I did okay: I felt comfortable with chores in the stockroom, hit it off well with the student help, held my own with the head office buyers, the suits with tiny cracks in their shoes. But at the front of the store, when the mike was handed to me and the button on its base depressed, I froze, couldn't get "Good Afternoon, Shoppers" out of my mouth.

Between jobs on newspapers, I'd harvested apples with Jamaican and Native American women who picked with two hands into their aprons, never bruising a Spy, a McIntosh.

I'd stacked Home Hardware catalogues in a print house; fitted plastic moldings on terminals in an auto parts factory; hoisted drywall sheets into the ceilings of chalets for the middle class. Each time I was fired or laid off, was told I was unacceptable. Until I found the job in Galt, as manager trainee of a drug department in a variety chain store, I was convinced that I'd never do anything right.

My stay in Galt was the only time in my life Father and I regularly exchanged letters. He wrote about product knowledge, advised me that I needed to know more than profit margins to get ahead. He counseled me to do my own research (on deodorants versus antiperspirants: Any age or sex pattern-buying? Seasonal ups or downs?), sent me articles from *Reader's Digest* about salesmanship, a long piece that claimed excessive use of a popular herbal shampoo could lead to premature hair loss. Letters came regularly, about one a month. Father pressed so hard when he put pen to paper that a blind man could trace the backs of the letters he sent to me and not miss a single word.

It came to me slowly, bit by bit, but soon I was passable on the mike. The secret, I found, was to stare into the wire mesh, never look up and be distracted by the cartpushers—wives, working women, grandmothers, or Harriet Neatby, the store sleuth. Other manager trainees learned the order books, organized the stock room, or filled understock shelving beneath the sales counters. But I took to writing and performing all the sales announcements—from tweezers to toilet rolls, the fifteen-minute specials, deals on German-made hair dryers in the center aisle.

As I yakked away, feeling more confident, I gradually lifted my eyes from the mike and observed the town—who lived there, what they bought. I learned to tell a lot about people from the underarm deodorant they picked up, knew at a glance who would select unscented, would insist upon Secret. It took a shopper of a particularly bold stripe to carry out Kotex in such bulk that no plastic bag could surround them, or take a chance on a new dandruff shampoo, a generic pain reliever. ("Shopping is destiny," I scribbled once in the margins of the order book.)

Before long, I became fascinated with the customs surrounding the buying and selling of condoms. In small towns, no other public measure of intimate life comes close.

From the elevated platform behind the cash register, I observed the shy, uncertain buyers, young men with darting eyes, a feather-weight box of condoms tucked in their armpit, while their girl stood in the back of the department pawing a bottle of shampoo. Then there were the tough guys who planted the box English-side up on the counter by the register and never raised their eyes. So cool.

Underneath, rested the latest copy of *Ring* or *Dirt Bikes and Dirt Wheels*. But their girlfriends, too, stood at the rear, holding a bottle of shampoo, ever so suggestively.

The shy, uncertain ones, the first-time buyers, left separately, arranged to meet their girlfriends outside long after the sale had been rung up. But the cool ones felt no such shyness: They stepped away from the cash register, their white and red Woolco bag held out front, grabbed the hand of their girlfriend in "Shampoo" and left. No muss, no fuss.

I studied the behavior of the buyers, the men, but it was the women I was drawn to. While sorting mint and plain Metamucil in the stockroom, counting the overstock of Brylcreem, I imagined their kisses. I had spent two years in college then, in Ottawa, a frigid city where the girls I wanted paid no attention to country boys like me. In the Galt stockroom, I imagined holding a pretty woman's hand forever, turning it over and over in my palm, lacing my fingers in and out of hers.

Galt girls whose boys bought condoms for them were in a fix. They couldn't stay in the car, it would attract suspicion. And they couldn't come to the counter, they would be seen. Staying in the shampoo section was best. Girls with shy and dubious boyfriends could slip a hair product their way and help cover the purchase if someone from the neighborhood or Bible class happened by. For the girl it was a perfect cover to stay at the back, examining the bottles of shampoo and conditioner.

If a guy was spotted on a summer evening carrying around a small bag from MacDonough's Drugs or Fennemore Pharmacy, what would people think? Anonymity was in the bag at Woolco. The bag could contain anything: polyester socks, a deck of cards, toothpicks, Kleenexes. I knew something of anonymity. Not knowing a soul in town, I became the preferred supplier of condoms. In one fifteen-minute period, with cashier Vera Fretter, a gossipy high-school cheerleader, on break, I once sold thirteen boxes of twelves, a total sale of $217.53—a personal best.

In a letter to Woolco International in the United States, I gave a full explanation of my condom-consuming theory for small towns. It was best if girls had a discreet place to go, most conveniently to shampoo. Under no circumstances move shampoo away from the back of the departments, I said.

One day at the drug department, a young man, no more than eighteen, walked to the cash register and plunked down a carton of forty-eight red-ribbed Centurions, a $24.99 sale. Vera was cashier; I was talking to Harold, the pharmacist on alternate Thursdays, a few steps away on the landing above.

The man looked like Opie of Mayberry, only taller. Later, Vera would say the girl beside him was local, but she didn't recognize him. I had my back to them at first, but I noticed her out of the corner of my eye. Her eyes were dark, lustrous, almost pleading. Dishwater brown hair. My heart sank when I looked at her, a little girl really, barely twelve I'd say, but at that moment I wanted her more than anything. She winked at me as her right hand moved out of sight toward the front of her partner's pants.

Opie paid cash with a twenty and a five and left behind the penny—and the bag and the receipt. Her eyebrows raised and mouth open, Vera held the penny between her thumb and forefinger above the register drawer as the stranger tossed the Centurions into the air like a peewee football. The girl's arm was looped around Opie's waist as the pair strolled out of sight.

That night I stayed in the store until daylight, working like mad, stripping the pain relievers, antacids, and cold remedies from the front of the department, putting them where I'd emptied the shelves of shampoo. Then I stacked the shampoo in shelves at the front of the department. The next day I put in my notice.

I had a thing about calling home, since my first night in Galt. I took the job in Galt in order to recover my strength after an illness. In a strange twist, I'd contracted a case of phlebitis, then a pulmonary embolism—a blood clot in my lung. I owed my life to an elderly bedmate whose name I can't recall, who for a week stayed awake through the night so he could press the emergency buzzer when my breathing stopped. Once, Father and Mum came to visit. They were shocked to see me in my wasted condition; in a little more than a month I'd lost thirty pounds, could barely lift my head off the pillow. They stood still, with tears in their eyes, silent, shuffling their feet. Outside of Keppel, they were nervous, disoriented, the young couple on the run in an outdated frame.

"We could stay," Father said to me. "Do you want us to stay?" He was afraid for me, I think, but there was a greater fear that I couldn't name. More than the anxiety of being in a foreign place, where once he was outside the hospital he would have to ask perfect strangers directions to a place where he would have to ask directions again. More than looking into the hollow, sapped eyes of his first-born son and recalling that other time, when the dying eyes were mine, too. The attending doctor was shaking his head. He is going to die, the doctor had said back then. It was a fear that stripped bare, brought him down to size. Standing there in the hospital, I realize now as I'm writing this, Father, for the first time that I'd known him, was defenseless. His whole life he hadn't gotten over something, and the renewed prospect of my death was bringing that terrible truth back. In ways that I'd never fully understood, he was still a child; and until that secret was revealed to me, I would be a child, too.

Father said he had to head on to suppliers in Montreal and pick up fireworks he couldn't get anywhere else. "Will you be all right?" he repeated. I knew that my doctor had assured him this time that I wouldn't die. "Sure, Dad," I said, looking away. "I'll be fine."

After leaving the hospital, I took some time off my studies at college and landed the job in Galt. I'd lost so much weight when I was sick that my clothes didn't fit me. Cheap ties hung around my collar like chromosomes. I couldn't bear to look at myself in the mirror, which was convenient, because the room I rented from a retired Italian woman didn't have one. There was a bed, an oversized bureau, floral wallpaper. The first night in Galt I bought a can of tobacco and cigarette papers and smoked rollie after rollie, until with each breath I felt sharp pains in my lung, until the smoke was so thick that I couldn't see the wooden crucifix tacked above the door.

The phone booth was on a busy intersection two blocks away where working-class dates cruised by in pickups and low-riding Chevies. "Run a mile for me" and "Keep your legs up" girls had cried, leaning out the window, as I'd jogged past them earlier in the day. My pace slackened to a walk; I felt like a husk, as though the wind could blow me away. Except for college, I'd never been away from home. I'd made, I was sure, a horrible mistake.

"Will you accept a collect call?" the operator asked.

"Sure will," Mum said. "How are you, son? We've been worried sick about you. Wondering when you'd call."

"I dunno," I said, tapping ash from the cigarette. "I'm just getting myself sorted out down here."

"So, how's it going?"

"Goin'? It's goin'."

"No, really."

"I don't know, it's a little too early to say."

"Well, y'know you can always come to us . . . I mean that. . . . So, tell me, can you get Jim's games on radio down there? It's the playoffs and the Griffins are doing better than expected. Of course, your father's biased, but he'll give you a earful as to the reasons why, even if the broadcasters won't. Listen in if you can. Eight o'clock start, I believe."

"Uh huh."

"Next time you're up, I'll tell you some TALL TALES. Tuesday Afternoon Ladies League and Thursday Afternoon Ladies Euchre Series. Those are our new names for our alley bowling and card-playing groups. Whaddya think? Can you believe it, they made me the secretary? Helen's fine, don't see her as often as we'd like. Here's your father. Now, call again soon, promise?"

Tires squealed; I imagined the working-class girls laughing at me—a boy from a country town, in polyester brown trousers, ears that stuck out too far in the fresh haircut I'd had for my first day at work. The booth's pale roof lamp flickered, threatened to go out.

"You're all right?" Father asked. He had been sitting in the La-Z-Boy, watching Jewish comics, scanning *TV Guide*.

I did not say I was as sad as I'd ever been, certain that I'd screwed up in my life. It was his view, not mine, that retail life was in my cards. That college was unnecessary. "Yup, I'm okay," I said in my practiced manner. Never let on. He was inquiring about my physical state, after all, I reasoned. I wasn't under mortar fire in a foreign city, a war reporter under siege. No broken bones, gushing blood vessels. My head wasn't severed and lying in the middle of the road. "Yup. Okay."

"Now's not the time to talk, then; I'll check with your mother for the details. You'll have your own phone soon, right? Home for Easter? Fine. We'll talk then. Good luck on the job." And then he hung up. I held the phone and listened as the line clicked off and the dial tone resumed.

Before entering my room that night, I heard the faint sound of voices on the second floor of my rooming house. It appeared to be coming from behind a door at the end of the hall, and walking closer, I heard a man's voice. "Go ahead. I've got you. Over." The next voice was Eastern European, I thought, civil yet insistent. "Please. Speak to my brother in Thunder Bay. I cannot get through. Mama dreamed of him last night. She wants to hear his voice. Over." The man behind the closed door asked for the call numbers, said he would do the best he could. He was hailing Thunder Bay as I turned to go to my room.

I lay awake that night on a gold bedspread with a pebbled design, vowing that I'd never again call my father, that if it could be done, I wouldn't even dream about him.

Jack London was like a bush pilot in one thing: his beginner's mind. London reveled in the lone, tiny flower against a background of tundra, the rainbow of light glistening on an icicle in the setting sun.

The writer spent only one winter of his life in the north, but his stories about that time were his truest, the best loved. His friend, Klondiker Emil Jensen, wrote:

"To him, there was in all things something new, something alluring, something worthwhile, be it a game of whist, an argument, or the sun at noonday glowing cold and brilliant above the hills to the south. He was ever on tiptoe with expectancy, whether silent with wondering awe, as on a night when we saw the snows aflame beneath a weird, bewildering sky or in the throes of a frenzied excitement while we watched a mighty river at flood-tide."

London was but a visitor to the north, yet bush pilots remain, Zeligs of the wilderness, taking on the character of the land.

Not long after I went to Windsor, I met a bush pilot at a wedding reception. "This is my cousin, the bush pilot," a friend had said. Only during a convention of dairy farmers I'd covered as a cub reporter had I felt such a powerful handshake. His hands were no larger than mine but his fingers were stubbier, thicker, like an orchard branch in winter.

Not knowing what to say, I told him a college friend I had come to like once went north to be a bush pilot. "Have you met him?" I asked, mentioning his name. "Not yet," the bush pilot said.

Drinks came and after a long draught and some more small talk I told him of my longing for the north. I'd read that bush pilots could simulate the sun's rising, not once but twice, by suddenly dropping altitude at daybreak, taking advantage of the curvature of the Earth. Had he sensed the charged air about the pole, the true north? What of the chants of the shaman, the magic of *quamaneq*? The colors of icebergs he had seen?

From above, the view of the north would be like a photo negative, all blacks and whites—polar bears against black water, black guillemots over snow. Leads in sea ice as seen from the air would resemble arteries, black coursing through white. Not only images reverse themselves. Spirit flows outside in, not inside out. A northerner's laugh is an exploding mine—powerful and unexpected. The pressure of it ignites all the air in the room.

"Being a bush pilot," he said, finally, smiling broadly, "is the life of Reilly." At first, he was shy, uncomfortable with so many people around, but I guess he took my nervous earnestness as an invitation to confidence because soon he was spilling his guts, laughing out loud, ordering beers all around.

He told me of cobalt glacial lakes seen by fewer people than pass through Times Square in a single moment; of once standing toe-to-toe with an adult grizzly—staring it down, until it passed, brushing his jeans to get by in the narrow break of the forest; of how polar bears stalk the near-sighted ring seal by covering their shiny nose with a paw to blend in with the white all around. Once a year the bush pilot visits a hermit trapper and eats steaks of polar bear and musk ox, washing it down with skunky beer, gone bad in the midnight sun. It's the only meal all year the trapper shares with anyone. The hermit asks: Who's president? AIDS—What's that? Does Jerry Garcia still tour?

The other wedding guests were dancing "the Hokey Pokey" (a reprise) when the bush pilot said, "You know, I've seen the narwhals, the sea beast with the horn. Once they thought 'em to be the unicorn, but they were mistaken. In those days, a narwhal tusk was worth ten times its weight in gold.

"They don't know anything about 'em, how many there is, their mating habits, whatnot. They know more about the stars. In ancient times they were thought to be mermaids, then a corpse at sea. A few too many narwhal tusks were found among real corpses, so stories of them got even more grisly. People just stayed clear.

"It was in Lancaster Sound between Devon and Baffin. I was traveling at about a thousand feet when I first saw a school of them, all sparkling electric blue in the April light. Eskimos have this saying, *Quviannikumut*, for feeling very happy, and that's what it was like for me.

"I went down then, a few hundred feet above the ocean, and there they were those little devils. They're the shyest animal known to man, not trusting like dolphins and whales, so to find them like this, in open water, torquing along, was really something to see.

"There were six of them: one male with a golden tusk—the color of gold, I mean—sticking out a dozen feet or more. The others were the blue of God's Oldsmobile. Beauty. From time to time, the male snuck underneath the baby, no more than three feet long, and flipped it clear out of the water, just for fun.

"I don't know whether the noise of the prop was getting to them or what, but just then the most amazing thing happened," he said, as he dug into his pocket for cigarettes. "I was drifting down another hundred feet, as close as I dared go, when the male leaped clear out of the water, all white and gleaming, like a swordfish on a line."

He paused, fumbled with cigarettes he'd pulled out of his pocket, and lit one. "Was it a warning, eh? a 'Get the hell out?' Or a final goodbye? I'll never know, but when that beast hit the water they all vanished as if they were never there. Poof, gone. 'Cause a foot down it's nothing, blackness, all out of view."

He reached out and touched my hand, while digging into his pocket once more. Then, from his clenched fist, he dropped in my open hand what looked like the top of a Softie ice cream cone done by a novice with not enough twist. But it was as solid as a ceramic insulator on a telephone pole.

"An Eskimo trader swapped this one for my hunting knife," he said. "I never go anywhere without it."

While the final song, *MacArthur Park*, played and the party broke up, I held the tip of the narwhal horn in my hand. I remained in the empty hall for hours that night holding it, talking to the bush pilot. My thoughts for the first time in what seemed like ages were on the cedar chest, my father's past, of how I couldn't escape it.

The winter I left Woolco I saw The Lights. Eskimos call them simply "The Lights," but we know them as aurora borealis, the northern lights, packed with the power of a trillion watts.

The people I was with didn't see them, but I did, or thought I did. "Up there, the crown of the night sky," I cried, pointing, "The northern lights!" But no one saw. For a moment they looked up, then declared me nutty and walked on. Once, at a powwow, the emcee in a baseball cap that said POWWOW FEVER interrupted the dancing to say an eagle was flying overhead. "Thank you Great Spirit for blessing us," he said. The Native Americans all pointed above to a single spot. I saw nothing, a speckless sky.

Eskimos say if you talk softly the northern lights will come near. Miles upon miles of threadbare colored ribbons turn slowly, over and over, never staying whole, breaking apart, forming, breaking apart again. Eskimo shamen once read in The Lights messages from ancestors long dead, or the karma of the unborn. They stood beneath them and wove long narratives of what was to come: fresh game for that year or a leader among men. They told of the first white men, of terrible famines, of boys who would be unfaithful as men, while others pounded skin drums, chanted the old songs.

I thought I heard whisperings, a breeze through a hollow. Explorer Samuel Hearne said the northern lights emitted a sound like a large flag flapping in the wind. But the sound I heard was not patriotic. It was a sacred murmur, a message locked in tonal abyss, beckoning, yearning.

The *Star*'s deadline clock tripped to 12:07 A.M. My Tim Horton's was cold. Father answered on the first ring.

"Thanks for returning the call," he said in his best salesman's voice.

"No problem," I replied in mine. "What's up?" I had picked up a story in need of a headline and was turning on the video display terminal.

"There's a lad in a bit of a spot and I wonder if you could help. He's a trucker on his way to the United States from the West who'll be coming your way." Trucking was Father's idea of serious business. He spoke gravely as he used to when Jim was off his game. Now a sales executive for Brewers' Retail with a wife and two kids, Jim was in his rookie season in the over-thirty leagues, in his good years, had the best plus-minus in Keppel Industrial.

The story I had pulled was an eight-inch squib, a two-line, one-column head. Eleven characters per line. A Mideast hostage rumor.

I liked writing headlines: first on sports, "BEARS MAUL LIONS," then district, "MRS. EGBERT FRETWELL WINS CASSEROLE CONTEST." For the psychic who when put under hypnosis lost her mentalist powers: "WOMAN HAS HALF A MIND TO SUE"; for the town crier who advanced to the national finals: "FOR CRYING OUT LOUD, HE DOES IT AGAIN"; the bus-fare evader who was collared and was found to have a severed finger in his pocket: "EVASION OF THE BODY SNATCHER"; and on the page where the jump appeared, "COPS FINGER FINGER."

"Anyway some Yankee job didn't come through until he was in Brandon," my father said. "They got word to him through the CB grapevine and he'd really like to take it, but he's got no money for meals. Fuel's no problem; he's got credit."

I could sense my father was nervous, that he needed something from me but was having trouble asking for it outright. But I wasn't going to make it easy. I was enjoying the sound of discomfort in his voice.

"Are you still there, boy?" my father asked.

"Sure," I said, shifting in my seat. The phlebitis left me with a stiff leg and occasional sharp pains. The hostage reported in the wire story was not a household name so I couldn't use it in the headline. "U.S. HOSTAGE/MAY BE FREED" was too long. And "HOSTAGE DEAL/RUMORED" too ordinary, would be rejected by the slot. I signaled the copy chief with both hands for permission to bump down the size of the head and get more characters per line and make it easier to write. She was not easily distracted from her own work, and I'd found the best way to get her attention was to wave like a signalman.

"We should have called you a bit sooner, I know, but I didn't find out about the problem myself until this morning and then I had to go to Toronto to pick up an order. . . . I've just gotten home."

The copy chief shook her head: "Everything stet tonight," she yelled in my general direction, before burrowing back into her tube. No changes allowed.

"He was in the Soo at 11 P.M. I gave his father directions to your place and he'll relay them to the driver. The boy's expected to be there about dawn. He'll just rest until you get there."

On the keyboard I tapped in headline coding and "HOSTAGE/ORDEAL OVER?" Not so good, I usually shunned question heads, but with such spex, what could they expect? "Who is the guy?" I asked.

"He's your cousin, son. My brother's boy."

"Oh," I said, amazed.

"One hundred dollars cash should do it. You can handle that, eh?"

" . . . Uh huh . . ."

"Well, that's all for now. Thanks again for returning the call." He gave me the license number, the make of the rig, and then my father hung up.

tracks

Solitude's a northern thing. Wolf kills show on tundra for up to four years, signs of caribou scat for thirty. Snow has been falling on the ice fields of Ellesmere for centuries, never melting.

An Eskimo once stood off-stage before a large crowd. The spectators were angry, stomping their feet and wringing their hands as the man in parka and mukluks walked alone on stage. Suddenly, the crowd fell silent. For a long time the Eskimo did not say or do anything but stand before the throng, his arms outstretched. After a long time, his arms fell to his side and he slowly turned around, still without making a sound or crying out, until his back was to the people and he was facing north.

Northerners learn to hold their tongue and by doing so lose touch with the civilized, said Susannah Moodie, the pioneer writer. Living in the wild she declared herself "no longer fit" for society. She grew "content to live and die in obscurity," to "cling to her solitude."

"Nothing but solitude" was how one Arctic explorer described the land that he saw.

The first thing I did to prepare for my cousin's visit that morning was to strip the red flannel bedspread from the front picture window of my apartment. Usually after the midnight shift, I'd keep the bedspread up and sleep until midafternoon. In winter, darkness fell at 4 P.M. and I'd spend the next hours reading and watching boats on the Detroit River and car traffic on the international bridge. Not merely Sin City, Windsor is also where the most international crossings are made day in and day out. In the hours before I went to work each night I'd take down the bedspread and watch the winding lines of red and white taillights on the bridge, beads on a celestial string.

With the bedspread down, I put my coffee cup on the window ledge to cool. A cartoon bubble of condensation formed on the glass. Like birds gathering before migration, trucks chose my street to congregate on before heading south. They lined the block, crept up the crumbling sidewalk. Genies of blue smoke rose beside mud-streaked Macks, Kenilworths, and names I didn't recognize.

Three Macks fit the description of my cousin's rig, so it wasn't immediately clear which one was his. In the gray light of dawn I couldn't make out the license plates except for the Kenilworth, a sleeper cab from Tennessee, directly out front. I took a sip of coffee. Too hot, burned as it went down. Arms akimbo, I leaned against the double pane, cradling the hot drink in my hands. Be like a private eye, I thought, a snoop. A role I'd fashioned from years as a newsman. When my coffee cooled off I would head out to find my cousin.

Ripples in black water. Narrow lines, wide apart. A seal moves slowly many feet below an air hole in sea ice. Above, a hunter waits. It could be the seal has slowed, is conserving strength. A yearling may not be able to hold its breath much longer. A gray beard would have sensed trouble, retreated to another opening in the ice.

The hunter kneels on the extra padding of wolf's ruff stitched in his sealskin leggings. Whale blubber is clenched in his teeth. Except for the wolf fur, hidden from view, the hunter is cloaked in animal hides of the sea. Slowly he stands, suspended like a puppet, the harpoon raised in his right hand while his left reaches back and holds the high-powered rifle with scope strapped to his shoulder. The rifle he uses for polar bear, caribou, musk ox. Seal is taken in the old way.

The hunter imagines the Maiden of the Deep in her underwater home, her long hair tangled full of game. The walrus, which does not live in these parts, is not on his mind. With each breath he feels more a part of his place, the edge of the sea.

A wave on water. The hunter lets fly the harpoon and bounds back, straddling coils of rope that are rapidly unwinding. Stuck deep in the seal's flesh, the harpoon goes down with the fleeing animal. The rope twists and jerks. The hunter winds the rope about himself and pulls. He pulls the rope ten, twenty, thirty feet, then the beast dives and the hunter loses balance, falls, and is dragged hard along the ice toward the air hole. A man tied to the back of a speeding midsize car. Again the man yanks on the rope, working the wounded seal through the water. With a vicious kick the beast revives, upsetting the hunter for a second time. Except for his face, which smashes into the jagged ice as he falls, cutting his lip, nose, and cheek, it's slapstick, a million laughs.

The two struggle in this way and an hour goes by. Finally, the seal dies of shock and exhaustion, and only his dead weight obstructs the capture. The hunter chops around the air hole, makes an opening ten times as large, and finally brings up the ring seal. A big one. A gray beard of many wars, judging from his scars.

Before the hunter skins the animal, he opens the dead seal's jaw and squirts some water inside. Life is a cycle; the water keeps it unbroken. No living thing is ever his to claim.

My everyday lumberjack shirt usually kept me warm enough, but there was a nasty chill in the air that morning. I pinched the collar with one hand and carried my coffee in the other. Caffeine and a north wind revived me like a slap. I had been on nights too long, and there seemed no hope of advancement. Around me were homely women who'd abandoned dating, reprobates, binge eaters. One man in the press room worked nights for thirty years, turned his private world upside down. While he was at work his wife cleaned the house and watched videos until he returned home at first light. They slept from 10 A.M. to 5 P.M., had breakfast at 6 P.M., lunch at 11 P.M. On vacations they took Red Eye flights to safe havens, beaches where they could walk and relax in the moonlight. Never sunburn. Today they're retired, living down south in the night.

I passed by the Kenilworth, on to the Mack, a Florida orange color. From the street you can't see inside. Just as well. Truckers are a queer lot; guileless, yet mean and surly, conspiracists, libertarians, escapees of one failure or another. The Mack reeked of diesel, had supine girlie reflectors on the mud flaps. A picture of Jack Nicholson, on the facing side of the blind pulled down in the sleeper cab, looking mean, pointing like Uncle Sam: "I QUIT SMOKING. YOU KNOW WHAT I MEAN?" The license didn't check. Alaska.

Pictures of silvery nudes are one thing, but truckers aren't the type to take kindly to lechers. Perhaps my father had a sordid past, I thought, recalling the desire in his eyes the summer we saw my cousin's sister, the sign girl. My trucker cousin will be powerful and nasty, a no-nonsense type who'll take the hundred bucks and beat me senseless, leave me for dead. "White trash!" he'll scream, pounding my head with his fists. "You're just like your father." He'll be for capital punishment, family values. But if so, wouldn't he resist at all costs coming here, the home of a sinner's son? He must be desperate, really down on his luck, stooping to take money from such kin.

The next Mack was down the block, near a Yellow Freight, a regular. Ontario plates. I could see a man waving his arms on the sidewalk. But he wasn't waving them at me. He wasn't even looking my way. He had dirty blond hair, a lumberjack shirt like mine but of a heavier fabric, baggy jeans. His wide stance looked like a cop's, and as I drew closer I saw that his arms weren't waving but swinging rhythmically at his side. Hands fluttered like birds. With each swing of his arms the man seemed to grow more still. Skating on freshly flooded ice I had felt calm and contented but this was deeper, protracted. As though the movements could go on forever.

He was lanky, not a lot to him—a skinny man, wiry. But even the smallest of working men show their strength in the forearms, thick arteries pushing blood to the hands. The rolled-up sleeves of his shirt brushed the side of his jeans as he exercised, giving off a soft, swishing sound.

Suddenly, he stopped and looked at me. "Hello," he said, adding my name. "Pleased to meet you, I'm John." For as long as I was watching him, he had been watching me. Normally, this would have bothered me, but John's manner was polite and disarming, and in my current hopeful state of mind, I thought, even beseeching. Perhaps there was something more than money that he needed.

When we shook hands, John's palms felt smooth, his pull easy. He popped a peppermint Life Saver in his mouth and he offered me one. I stooped to put my coffee on the curb and while peeling back the paper, he said, "Man, you can't believe it. Really, it's too much."

"What's that," I said, then "Christ!" loudly, as I dropped the candy, my fingers numb from the cold.

"Don't worry about it, cousin," he said, pressing his hand firmly on my back. He dipped into his pocket and offered me a Life Saver from another roll while grinding the fallen ones under his boot. The candy tasted sweet, made me even more light-headed.

"It's cold," said Cousin John, shouldering a worn rucksack. "Let's get inside."

A wall of heat hit us as Cousin John and I entered the apartment. Windows in the front didn't open so it got stuffy in winter. I offered

John breakfast, but he said no, yawned deeply and snatched a game puck from the Grey Devils I kept on the mantel and flopped down on the sofa.

"Were you there the night Bill Fleming died?" he asked, fingering the Devils insignia. My white cat, which had disappeared in the place for days, nudged John's ankle, wound in and around his legs, and looking bored, wandered away.

"No . . . but my dad and brother were," I said. "Say, what did you mean when you said . . ."

"Helluva a hockey player . . . Listen, I don't know about you but I can hardly keep my eyes open. I've been driving all night and . . ."

"Sure, I understand, just . . ."

"Then I do my tai chi and that totally relaxes me. And with this heat blasting in here."

"I'll turn it down."

"Do that. And if it's all the same to you I'd like to catch a little shuteye. Down sheet lane, you know."

"Sure John, but . . ."

"Listen," John said, propping himself up on an elbow. "I'll bet your old man said that I was in a hurry. . . . Well I'm not. Not really. Let's take some time, get to know each other. Later."

I said sure, okay, if you put it that way. He asked me for a blanket and in the time it took me to go to the linen closet and back, Cousin John was fast asleep.

Moose do not roam aimlessly from place to place. Neither do caribou. Hunters live to know where these beasts go and why. Hunters track moose and caribou. Spouses track lemmings and foxes. Families track the hunter. A rolling stone gathers no moss, but who the hell eats moss? If you stay in one place you die.

"What amazes me is how accommodating the road can be," Cousin John said, his arms draped on the back of the sofa, his legs resting on my steamer trunk that doubled as a coffee table. He had been awake for a few hours, making small talk: the weather, jobs, Teamsters.

"Actually, exhibits change pretty regular at the Cowboy Hall of Fame. Parking is right off the interstate, special section for rigs. WHAAAAAAA? Country and Western? You don't dig it? One day you'll come with me and we'll hit some open stretch of road, and crank up 'I Put My Life on the Center Line' or some classic Waylon. You'll be hooked for life . . . I keep a notebook of the signs I see, a catalogue of wacky wonders, I call it. 'Microwave in Use; American Indian Visitors Center; Hungry Mother State Park; Your Last Rest Area; Hitchhikers Could Be Escaping Inmates.' You've heard about traveling across the Heartland of America? Well don't believe it. For twenty-odd years or more it's the 'Waistline of America' we've been criss-crossin'. When Elvis left the building so did that old-time America."

As a gag, when I first moved to Windsor, friends sent a vacuum cleaner salesman over to my apartment. The man had sat on my new sofa and talked freely, just as Cousin John was doing. The salesman, yapping a blue streak, spilled cookie crumbs on the thin broadloom and sucked them up with his machine. I settled on a hideaway vacuum with extra attachments. He stayed the rest of the day and for a while until he moved to the suburbs we would meet at Tiger Stadium for baseball.

"There you go again," John said, shaking his head. I was rubbing hard the palm of my right hand. "I saw it outside and again now and I can hardly believe it. Nana used to do that with her hand. Outside with the candy, and now the way you're sitting, rubbing your hand just the way she used to do."

"Who's Nana?"

"Why, our grandmother."

"Wha . . . but I didn't . . ."

"You know, that's all it is . . . just the way you make this little gesture, you remind me of her, that's all."

"But, I don't know anything, John," I said, my voice rising to a shout. "You must know I don't know anything."

"Uh huh, I guess I knew that." Then he grew silent. I pressed him for more information, but his eyes glazed over. He had turned inward as he did on the street, doing his tai chi. Cousin John was a talkative man, but my heart sank when I sensed he might tell me nothing at all.

If Magritte were Eskimo the landscape would be the mind, the objects not the middle class with umbrellas, but animals of their dreams, the spirit track.

Unlike the middle class, for whom life is a series of repetitions, Eskimos engage the world with a beginner's mind: the new not an empty phrase but a living thing. The best hunters follow the knowledge handed down for centuries, listen to their instincts, trust their dreams.

Their trails aren't clear pathways, a permanent route, some Santa Fe Trail of the north. Eskimo tracks are mental maps. They never take the same route twice. Hunters' dreams not only tell the location of game but the route to take. Visions reveal the site where a brother once shot a polar bear or the cove where walruses have migrated. They also see the birth of a future son, a shipwreck from years gone by. To forsake a hunting vision risks angering the Maiden of the Deep, bringing famine upon the people.

When the way is obliterated by whiteout or fog, an Eskimo in summer travels along sea ice, steering a course between the squawk of seabirds on the coast and the sound of the surf below. Over stormy terrain obscured like vaseline on glass, he holds course by watching the angle of the wind as it cuts swaths in the soft fur of his clothing. He reads the ground underfoot—the depth, spacing, and direction of the ridges—for clues to the thickness of the ice.

Eskimos follow visions but they are not dreamers. They are the most practical of people. A family on the hunt packs up and carries only the essentials—a harpoon, snow knife, needles and thread, caribou hides, a cooking pot. Other things will be found along the way.

In camp, northerners will appear sullen, sluggish, even stupid, lazing on a worn sofa, smoking roll-your-owns, sucking lemon drops. They can be silent for days, even weeks. Then they go on the hunt. Words come slowly, then with ease, until you cannot get them to stop. It is not so much a burst of energy but a tapping of it. Like an unused pipe warming with fresh heat.

That night I called in sick and Cousin John and I went drinking. "Let's just have fun," John had said, "get to know each other. Nothing heavy." It was a few days after The Canadian Caper in Iran, the American hostage event that gave career diplomat Ken Taylor his own entry in the *Canadian Encyclopedia* and the right to name his price on the dinner club circuit. We drove across the border at Detroit to a dance bar on the waterfront. Canadian flags flew on telephone poles along the route to the bar; the Red Ensign flew at the main branch of the public library. American Embassy officials had been held hostage for so long even the barstools had yellow ribbons. Tonight, I thought, someone would buy us some beers.

"Hey! Canadians? Let me buy you guys a drink," said a man in a red-checked jersey. John and I joined the man and soon others in discount jeans and bad haircuts came around. "You'll remember this night for the rest of your life," another said. It truly was a miracle: Canadian dollars were being redeemed at par.

"C'mon back sometime. Better yet, come to my house for dinner," a tall man said. Phone numbers were written onto bits of paper and pressed into my hands. More drinks were passed our way. I smiled, said thank you for the drinks, thank you but no to dinner. The good-looking women were few and all taken, so we relaxed and got drunk.

From a window at the bar you could see the Detroit River and Windsor, a mile or so beyond. The lights of freighters winked back.

Not that long ago a car was being winched from the black water of the river as I was coming home late from my night off. I couldn't look upon the river and not think of that night.

Patches of scum lay across the surface of the car. In the light of the pickups and sedans that had stopped, the car looked intact, a macabre plaything, a shiny wet toy spinning in air.

The cop the news wags called "Constable Friendly," a guest columnist for the *Star* who wrote about safeguarding cottages and keeping snow boots in the trunk, came toward me, shaking his head. "You missed 'er, son." At night all cops look alike, their faces shadows on stone. "Off the record, it was a suicide drive. There are no tracks on the road; no brakes. He went about eighty miles per hour into the drink, saying goodbye with a splash."

I took some photographs at the site, recording the details, the boy's name and address, thanked Constable Friendly, and returned to the car. In my car sat a young woman I was seeing. With a camera around my neck and notepad tucked under my arm, I squeezed into the driver's seat and turned off the rock 'n' roll station on the radio. The words felt like lead in my mouth when I repeated the driver's name, said that it looked like he had killed himself.

She stared at me, her mouth agape, and screamed, "Not Steel! Not him!" and then began to weep. I drove down the highway, keeping a close eye on the speed, both hands on the wheel. Between sobs she said he had been an oddly quiet one, a boy with a sweet smile. "Steel," an ironic nickname. Strange and nervous with women, but sexy somehow, a lonelyheart. "I feel responsible," she said. "If only

I had known him a little better, perhaps this wouldn't have happened. Perhaps all he needed was a friend."

"But it's not your fault, love," I replied. I steered off the pavement, stopped the car and pulled her close, feeling suddenly amorous. "There, there," I said, and turned the radio back on to soft rock. She grew more composed, and we kissed. But then the first notes of "Only the Good Die Young" started playing and before I could turn off the radio for good, she started crying more bitterly than before.

On the Canadian side only the Holiday Inn was lit as we drove the waterfront road. "I'm ready to talk about it when you are," I said, finally, breaking the silence. "But if you want to be alone with your thoughts until you're ready to talk, I'll respect that too."

My date was twenty-one and beautiful but in the dim light of the dashboard she looked like a child. She had stopped crying, was dabbing her eyes with a balled-up Kleenex. With one hand on her lap, the other moving monotonously to her lips, she smoked one cigarette after another and stared blankly out of the passenger window. I asked her if she would rather go home. She shook her head. When I asked if she wanted to keep driving around, she nodded yes.

An hour went by. The lights of Detroit—the new Renaissance Center, Joe Louis Arena, business towers—and freighters on the river shone on the windshield, fell on our faces. Nowhere else along the Seaway, from Thunder Bay to the Gulf of St. Lawrence, do the freighters move so cautiously as through this narrow waterway. Nowhere is the contrast between the carnival of America and the collectivity of Canada so great.

Where was the terror? The pity? I had been at the scene of the tragic death of a young man, a friend of a woman I thought I cared about. But instead of feeling sad and compassionate toward her, I felt only desire. And not much of that. Somewhere a voice deep inside of me was crying to be heard, but I had no words for it. Nothing. Except for the hum of the tires on pavement and my date's tiny noises of inhaling and exhaling of cigarettes there wasn't a sound.

Fly-speckers, the old-timers called those working on the rim, the outer reaches of the news desk. Insects buzzing over the carcass of news—the surface of things. For me, it was the same with women: with woman after woman, I felt only physical, empty desire for their bodies, nothing more. I winced at the thought that once a woman would turn to me and ask, "What else is it you want? What do you feel?" That was the real terror for me because I had nothing to say— only secrets and lies. Open cabinets and lights that went on but never off.

"Can you stop and buy me some cigarettes? I'm just about out, then I'd like to go home," my date said at last.

At a twenty-four-hour place I knew, I told the cashier to put all the Du Maurier cigarettes she had into a bag and I paid for them and left. When I got back into the car, I put the bag between my legs and pressed the handrest buttons to open the windows. I shoved the bag of countless packs of Du Mauriers into the woman's terrified face and then hurled the bag and its contents into the night.

At the waterfront bar I was very drunk, hardly able to stand, and when "Last Dance" by Donna Summer was playing, I told the people who were sitting around me that I had something to say, something that I wanted to announce. Those who heard my request must have gotten the manager's attention because soon the music stopped, and all the lights went up. Boos ended quickly when the DJ said, "Hold it! Hold it! We'll crank it back up. From the beginning. But there's a Canadian at the bar who wants to say a few words." Everyone was clapping and two burly fellows escorted me toward the lighted dance floor, a swath of blue, green, and yellow lighted squares, to the booth where the DJ, a skinny man with hollow cheeks and dark glasses, smiling for all he was worth, handed me the microphone.

What is a traitor if not a man sickened by false faith? I was repulsed by the earnestness of the handshakes, the heavy pounding on my back. I had such rage in me—hatred of the ugliness of patriotism, the chauvinistic stain. But the roots of the anger weren't about that.

At the steps of the DJ's booth I turned and looked out over the crowd, a Saturday night throng, charged with lust and cheap booze. I paused for what seemed a long time to watch as the tobacco smoke swirled in the colored lights. Soon everyone was quiet and staring toward heaven as well, when into the mike I declared, clearly and distinctly, in my best Woolco voice: "THE AYATOLLAH WAS RIGHT!"

A look of recognition crossed Cousin John's face before he rushed to get me out of there and save my life. The people stared for a beat or two. They looked blank, like sheep.

Eskimos are known to kill deviants, those who repeatedly do not conform. The Tlingit will banish offenders, send them to distant, barren islands. In recent years two teenagers were banished to such a place for attacking and permanently injuring a pizza man. Northerners will tolerate aberrant behavior, put up with someone who keeps pulling against the better interests of the group. But the patience can wear thin. Two priests were once killed when they tried to make Eskimos take a journey they judged too dangerous to attempt, and years ago a trader who tried at gunpoint to force Eskimos to sell fox pelts to him was killed for being so obnoxious.

The next day I awoke, a cold compress on my head. John leaned over me and touched my hand. He was holding a sketch of mine, one of the international bridge I'd started. I'd recently returned to drawing, and the bridge was a favorite subject of mine. The span was a single stroke of dark, heavy pencil, then I'd cross-hatched the shadows with a fine tip. The arc was what interested me, not the ends.

"You were a maniac out there," John whispered as he fingered the drawing, shaking his head. "A fucking maniac," he said. "You could have got us both killed." John had whisked me out of the bar and into my car before anyone could get their hands on me. Or so John said. I couldn't remember a thing after what I'd said on the dance floor. My head was a makeshift shelf for a ton of bricks. It would only hold up if everything stayed still.

John had made a pot of coffee and placed a steaming mug on my bedstand. "You keep going like this you're going to be dead," he said an eyelash away from my face. He smelled of tobacco, stale beer, and Brut. The stubble of his beard buckshot in red flesh; his eyes cold and gray, unyielding in the way he could see right through me. I knew as I looked up at him in my weakened state that John was right. What was the basic instinct? To live close to the edge, to court disaster? Nothing mattered. What was family, faith? Endless secrets, only lies that bind. I had turned my back on my family, learned to respond like my father, the master of silence and brute force. But in the end I would not be that person. I was not my father.

"John," I said, with tears in my eyes. "Before you go, you must tell me . . . you must tell me what you know."

Grandmother loved to draw, John told me. Where she grew up, her artwork was prized by neighbors and people from away. She did birds mostly, gray birds, grouse, blackbirds on the wing. It was only later she did landscapes. In his rig, John kept a postcard-size print, a reproduction he attached to the underside of the sun vizor. The sun had weathered the picture and lines of indentation pressed down where a clip had held it in place. Formless, dark shapes were arrayed in no particular order. Winter trees, textured as if the medium were mud. Yet translucent, the confusion of flames.

Folks in Whitewater, Saskatchewan, framed little Ida Mulrany's perfect objects: family dogs, sunsets, still lifes. Her bowl of fruit, horse's head, and prairie shack hold central places in the homes of people where the *Farmer's Almanac* and the Bible never leave the bed-stand and the Salvation Army band plays on Saturday nights. In the bottom corner of each picture, with straight lines and hard angles, belying the soft, round artist herself, Grandmother had signed her name: LITTLE IDA.

Little Ida had an elder sister, Kathleen, and four brothers who would never marry, never leave home. Her mother died not long after Ida was born, and then her father vanished, too, never heard from again. In the only photo that survives of that time, Kathleen is an imperious raw-boned beauty in bare feet on a dirt floor. In the dress I'd seen before, the one she had worn in the picture hidden in my father's cedar chest, is Little Ida, books clutched to her chest. The boys are square-jawed, rheumy-eyed, yet all their looks are so fierce, so defiant, that I recognize Father in them instantly.

Kathleen had girls, four of them. They're retired now. Two live in trailers, another in a tract house in Kamloops, British Columbia; the fourth married well, taught school in Hope. They grew old telling stories of growing up in the Depression, of the dirt-floor cabin where they suffered through winter after winter, went sometimes days without food, and then only rolled oats, bits of meat in soup. Boys with a chance to make it on their own would have been forgiven if they'd have left, times were so desperate. But there were only girls and they all stayed, and somehow, survived.

But Ida, they said, would do more than just survive. With her natural skill in art, her love of books and learning, she could be whatever she wanted—a doctor, a lawyer, a painter. She could get a chair at an art gallery, a seat with an orchestra.

In Saskatchewan, the Mulranys made little or no profit each year on their sales of wheat and rye, but what coins and odd bills there were went into a large jar left in the kitchen. FOR LITTLE IDA, a sign said. By the time she was ready to go east at nineteen, to a Catholic college in Windsor, Ontario, and study art, the jar contained three hundred and twenty dollars, and because of her excellent studies, a letter from the school board to be redeemed for a scholarship of two hundred more.

Prayers linger in prairie skies. A clutch of nine Mulranys stood on the windblown platform in Tern, Saskatchewan, and watched as the train carrying Little Ida rolled toward her new home in the East. They knew in their hearts that day that Ida Mulrany would never return.

More than any other picture, Kathleen cherished Ida's oil painting of the grouse dance spectacle. It hung beside the crucifix, above the radio set, the place of honor.

People who study the prairie bird say their group celebrations, particularly during the spring, are similar to the earliest Native American dance rituals. On prairie grass, flattened like snow in preparation for a backyard rink, the grouse dance and wheel about, cry a near-human call. It is the only time all year that they make such a sound.

In Nana's painting, two birds throw back their heads, the ruff and wings blurred in a frenzy of movement. A bird in the foreground has human eyes. Dark, evil eyes that suggest disaster.

Grandfather always had a pencil ready. He kept no more than a stub behind his right ear, and in a flick of the wrist he drew solid lines on soft timber, wee circles, shorthand measurements only he could discern. Lucas O. was a worker at Windsor College, the senior carpenter of a small team that hammered studs for the new science building, when he first saw Ida. She had long, blond locks, a shapely body that filled out her cloth coat, an Eaton, mail-ordered from Regina. A cross at her throat. A grown man nearly twice her age, Lucas laid his coat on a sawhorse and offered Ida a seat. "I'm here every day," he said. "Drop on by when you're free." Then he doffed his bill cap, and walked back to work.

Occasionally, Lucas smiled at Ida, but mostly he worked with slow purpose, putting up the building piece by piece. After a while, Ida stayed for hours, with a drawing pad, later an easel, to capture the hard point of his cheekbone, the deep-set eyes, the bushy eyebrows. She began bringing him lunch, hot soup when the weather turned, hunks of bread slathered with spicy mustard. Once when it rained she had no protection and Lucas implored her to go home. Finally, she did, and as she lay awake that night she became convinced that more than anything else in the world, she wanted to marry this man. As a girl she used to have nightmares of being trapped in a deep well, unable to breathe. She'd reach up and there'd be nothing, no light, no air. That night without Lucas she had the girlhood nightmare again, and she knew that if she didn't have this man her life would be over. That rainy night in Windsor, Ida couldn't sleep so she worked at the drawing table, trying again and again to get the bill cap right, the line of rain droplets that glistened as his eyes did when Lucas smiled.

Nana would draw the boats in winter. She preferred the simple lines of the vessels, not the crew, so winter was best. In the cold, men worked in the holds, rarely went on deck. The wind was so great that more than one deckhand had been swept overboard and drowned in heavy coats and boots. In the background was Belle Island, where an old mansion stood amid trees hundreds of years old. From the Windsor shore, she sketched boats steaming north, toward the heart of America, to Detroit.

There was no escape from the wind, but from her seat on a boulder near shore Nana could get the best view. Folks walked by and shook their head or circled their index finger at their temple. But the woman pregnant with my father seemed not to notice; she sketched Belle Island and the boats without batting an eye.

Hours would pass this way and then she went home. Lucas was due to return from his new job, on a line checking that liquor filled to bottlenecks. In the Depression, building had slowed, you had to take what you could get. After opening the door to the small house, Nana passed by the crucifix, a secondhand easy chair, a throw rug, half-done paintings. From the window, only a corner of the kitchen could not be seen. There she bent down to free the knots she had tied, securely but not painfully, about the feet and hands of her first-born son, Lyall.

The Catholic church in Keppel was on the highest point of land, overlooking the failing restaurants in the harbor. In winter we tobogganed down slopes on Catholic land but we never climbed to the top, never went close to the church, its limestone steeple. Or the school attached. Neither did we go to the dark, spooky mansions in town or the abandoned houses that lined the base of the escarpment. Looking up from the harbor at the Catholic church and its school, I thought of a castle, a settlement guarded, but beyond its white cross above the door of the school, I did not know what lay.

At the Christmases I've imagined at Uncle Lyall's house, Nana always arrives late. A handsome woman with magnificent snowy hair, she puts linen envelopes in the tree for her grandchildren: "Merry Christmas—Love Nana" and a crisp five-dollar bill, so blue it could break your heart. Every year her leather gloves are a little less soft, more worn. Never does any flesh show, but in the end the covering would be very thin.

The rustle of petticoat; gleam of black polished shoes. My cousins, Mary and little Kay, don't flinch. They sit with legs crossed at the ankles in lace dresses on kitchen chairs arranged along the perimeter of the living room. At first I don't think the girls are real, rather like prize dolls in a giant dollhouse, but when I step into the room, they rise and come toward me, lead me to a kitchen chair beside them, and we all sit down. Kay has a tiny mole above her lip that darkens when she smiles. As she sits with her white-gloved hands resting in her lap, I am amazed at how still she could be.

Aunt Ruth's black hair is like a stained-glass figure's, bright and solid. Pasty-faced and stout, a farmer's daughter, and as yet the next baby doesn't show. Mum, in her burnt-orange dress that bunches at the waist, sits next to Lyall, eyes in a burrow. Shine a torch inside to tell the color.

Father shifts in his seat, and his elbow makes an amoeba of the doily on the armrest. Lyall leans forward and barely above a whisper tells my father it is okay. Please be comfortable.

Without warning, Nana gets up to leave. Bye-bye. Merry Christmas, all. No, don't get up. I said No. Her snowy locks stand out against her black cloth coat and fake fur collar. Boots like shiny raven's wings. Nana's eyes are fleeting, too, hidden. She looks but doesn't touch. Perhaps she is not there after all, but then there is the evidence. The lapis five-dollar bill in the linen envelope. Stack them up, year after year, the solemn Queen, with her Beatrice-Beauty-Salon-style hair. The never-changing image of the Queen herself. She stands on guard of our hearts. To hold and protect.

Just above my kitchen chair on the wall are the soles of Christ. The only crucifix in the room. The nail goes in below the ankle so the feet splay from the mount. I can't believe as I look at Christ's feet how smooth they must be to the touch. Not at all like an adult man's foot, with wrinkles and calluses, but like a newborn's, untouched by the world, someone's vision of what a foot could be. In that foot is the desert floor after a wind, the underside of a fresh pea husk, and before I know what I'm doing, I'm up from the chair, caressing the foot of Christ in my uncle's house. Before my father and Uncle Lyall can pull me away, put me in the spare room where I could do no more harm, I stroke the feet of Christ one by one. I find I can't help myself. I would've caressed his whole smooth, suffering body from head to toe if they hadn't got me out of there.

I had to get away. I remember now. On Sundays, Father never came home until late. And then he did, and so what? What is the sound of an empty room? House noises, the call of a wind-up bird. But no, in Keppel the crows have driven out all the birds that sing. Crows are smart, the ultimate survivors, fierce yet cowardly when pressed. But they cannot sing.

I'm a young boy in my room, waiting. Again, for something to happen. Always like that. In winter, I'm watching my father flood the rink, in summer, waiting for Father to come home. There's a radio on. "Hot, another scorcher, today." The radio needs to tell me that because I cannot feel the heat. Numb, as if my head is wrapped in gauze. What does the paper say? What's the temperature? Houses hold—and suffocate. Don't feel. Don't let the outside in. "But the heat has not damped the spirits of the Lion's Club Beach Walkers. They are on their way to Sauble Beach in a walk to benefit Keppel's church charities. Twenty-six miles under TODAY'S SUN. WHEW!"

I make a clean getaway. I could've said that I was skulking around, waiting for Mum to go downstairs with the laundry basket, for Jim to go to the bathroom, for Helen to take a nap. But that is not how it happened. If the Lion's Club could walk to the beach, then damnitall a nine-year-old kid could walk to the beach. I snap off the radio. Finally, something is happening. I am going to do something on my own.

I love being on the road. The sun on my face. The crunch of gravel. The sound of chewing sugared cereal. That never ends.

Maybe there are wind-up birds out here. Songbirds that would accompany the percussion of my footsteps. Around the next corner perhaps. Not? Oh well, I've got nothing but time. It's hot but that's okay. When it's hot, let me be hot, when it's freezing cold, let me freeze. I'm not hungry. I have my cereal. Road food.

The only way out of Keppel is along Sunset Strip. Seventy-Seven Sunset Strip, ba-da-dum. Seventy-Seven Sunset Strip, ba-da-dum. In the backseat of my father's car, we would parrot the song from the TV show, a late-night jingle we hear through the floorboards of the insul-brick house. Seventy-Seven Sunset Strip, ba-da-dum. In

L.A., the home of the program, it's the end of the line. What can exist beyond Seventy-Seven Sunset Strip? Over the cliff and into the sea.

In years to come, out-of-towners will come to Sunset Strip and build donut shops, fast-food hamburger joints, and a mall, with acres of free parking, miles and miles of poured concrete and asphalt sealing up for good the bottles, the beautiful amber and blue ones, with little etchings, stars and snowflakes, the beer bottles, the cherished ones my grandfather had promised to dig up for me.

But when I was nine years old there was only a bowling alley. With five pool tables. Not the end of the line, the beginning. Home of TALL TALES, the best twofer in town. Where once, long ago, the Canadian Amateur Snooker Champion played—and lost. Parking for twenty. No asphalt. Crunch, crunch, only gravel. And three- and four-room houses. With long laneways, and abandoned cars like so many boulders on either side of the lane. Great for hide and seek. Pry up the rear seat, springs and all, and jump in, separate the cushion and pull it down on top—tight. Ollie, Ollie, Ants and Free. Stay in there forever. No one would ever find you. Why don't you kids go outside and play. Hide and seek. Vanish. Disappear.

Get the hell out of our lives.

Perhaps they won't ever find me. The boy who wasn't supposed to make it, the sickly, odd, quiet one. They have called and called and I've not returned as I always have. Could I have fallen down the storm drain? Been cornered and attacked by Brandy, the St. Bernard? Wasn't it just the other day that a boy had been run over by a car, suffered permanent head damage? They say he'll have to live the rest of his life in a wheelchair, his arms as twisted and useless as drift-wood. A good, responsible boy would've never let it get this far, wandering away from home without giving a single thought to what this was going to do to his sweet Mum, his mind filled with nothing but idle thoughts of wind-up birds and the cereal-crunch of gravel while scanning the scrub land of scrawny pines and glacial boulders for a good place to begin digging. To begin looking for bottles.

The phone ringing in the dark startled me awake. How long had I been out? Where was John? Ow, my aching head. Oh, please, stop ringing. Hell, but it won't. It fucking won't. With each ring, it feels as though my head will explode. A hot boring tool liquefying my brain. E-coli poisoning. "LOCAL EDITOR'S BRAIN EXPLODES." With each step across the floor my head racks with pain, but I have to get to the phone. Stop the killer ring.

"'lo," I said.

"Yo." It was K. "Thought you'd never get up."

"What time is it?" I asked.

"Seven."

"Morning or night?"

"Whoa, baby, are you fucked up or what."

"Listen, it was either pick up the phone or die."

"Aren't you getting a little old for this?"

I hung up. Whatever it was it would have to wait. John was gone, that seemed clear. I groped my way back to the couch on my hands and knees and lay back, exhausted. Even the cat was gone. I'd not seen her since that first day with John. I'd inherited the white cat, she came with the place, so I'd never named her, never laid claim to her. My landlord was crazy for cats. His cat, Max, was the ugliest creature I had ever seen. Max lived upstairs in an abandoned apartment with broken windows and one working faucet. The cat was 42 years old, the landlord claimed. He had a single patch of gray ruff on an otherwise hairless body, one working eye full of a viscous fluid, and a hellish scream. Like nothing on earth.

The white cat was special, too. People come and go, but the cat stays. One tenant tried to take the cat with him when he moved to his own place in Toronto, but within days the cat had fled his adopted home. A week later, a starving, dirty cat arrived at the apartment house on Victoria Avenue, slipping in unnoticed as the new tenant went out to work that day. When the tenant returned, he found a clean white cat who leaped into his lap and purred so sweetly that the man was instantly enchanted. He, too, a year or so later, would take the cat away, even give it a name, something like Apollo or Antigone, but again it fled that place and returned home.

But now, it seemed, the cat was gone. Max would soon die and I would be alone.

I have a dream. I am doing well in a hockey game, shooting the puck with authority. Then, at a crucial moment, when I have to pass the puck up ice, it goes astray off the heel of my stick. As I chase it, I do so in great pain, and I find a fungus embedding into the flesh of my face. I stop and try to pull the fungus out with my fingers. But

I can't do it because my hand has become exposed muscle, sinew, burned flesh.

I do nothing and the pain stops. Then as I watch my hand gradually turns into a bar code, then a downhill ski pass. The pass is good for one day only, February 16.

The day the cat finally came back a small envelope was in the mailbox. Postmarked Keppel. No return address. I ripped open the letter and a yellowed clipping fluttered out. Attached was a Post-It that read: "Thought this might be of interest. John." The clipping itself was small, a filler. It read:

AREA FARMER DIES

Crawford's Mill reported the sudden death of Medford Road farmer, Lucas O. Police and hospital attendants were called to the scene, but at press time had nothing further to report.

thaw

The card catalogue of the Windsor Public Library was being over-hauled. And about time. The *Star* had done stories about the head librarian, a believer in high-tech, satellites, and self-help software programs for literacy. Prepare for the new age, she said. Dressed in a smart-looking blouse, her hair pulled back, she looked fetching in the Saturday feature photo, her face above her crossed arms atop the library's new computer. But Vera Hoffman had her work cut out for her. Change did not come easily in Windsor. No single issue in the three years I had worked at the *Star* drew more protest letters than the Toronto-born librarian's plans to put online the library's hold-ings and trash the card catalogue.

I kept the yellowed clipping in the envelope and put it in a folder. I'd researched a thousand stories, from prison Go-Boys to blue-ribbon schools. Now, finally, I'd work on the story of my life.

I'd guessed my grandfather had died when my father was young. In the thirties, maybe. But when had farmers stopped going to sawmills? Around Keppel, the bush had been thinned of its best timber, but many farmers maintained a stand of trees, a few acres or so. They still go to sawmills today. In the townships around Keppel things haven't changed in fifty years. Probably never will. Newspapers go to electronic pagination, ending careers of printers, typesetters, and paste-up artists. Electronic cameras make dark-rooms obsolete, idle photographers. On a desktop, a four-color book with 3-D photos is around the corner. But farmers around Keppel still go to sawmills.

The clue to its age was in the quality of the type. Within the words themselves some of the letters looked different: the Rs in "Crawford" were of different weight, one was slightly off-center. Printing like this predated Linotype, which was first to give a single straight line of type—it had to be hot lead. The paper itself was not only yellow but fragile to the touch. Its edges were crumbling like ash, so I placed it back in the envelope. The mid-thirties, I said, to the librarian's assistant the next day after finding the clipping in the mail. Do you have on electronic file copies of the *Keppel Advance* from the mid- to late thirties?

He said no, but he would check with the librarian about an electronic share. Keppel's library was in the network, so in this case perhaps it was possible. "I wonder could you give it special atten-tion," I said. "I work at the *Star* and this is a priority for us."

The assistant said he would do what he could and walked off, glad to have a job to do. A *Time* magazine and a *Maclean's* lay on the countertop. "HOSTAGES, MISSING IN ACTION," the *Time* cover said. The alleged terrorist was wrapped in a kaffiyeh. The eyes burned. The *Maclean's* cover was a Bronze Age man found entrapped in ice on a mountain. Scientists were hailing it as the most significant discov-ery of its type. The Iceman had been born forty centuries ago and was mummified by wind and preserved in ice, wore weatherproof clothing of leather and fur lined with hay. A bronze axe was at his side. I tossed *Time*, then tucked *Maclean's* under my arm and went to look for the assistant.

"The librarian will see you now," the aide said. "Just go right in."

Vera Hoffman, a swirl of golden fabric about her neck, did not look up when I came in. "Just take a seat—I'll be right with you," she said, staring into a computer console, tapping at speed. Her hair was thick, piled high, dark chocolate scraped with a garden rake. The room smelled of apricots. While she worked, I read of the Iceman, feeling more than a little sick.

"We help a lot of *Star* people," she said, as she closed her pro-gram and turned to face me. She had deep brown eyes, a small smile. "Mostly with real estate, business dealings, the United Way—that sort of thing. . . . It's refreshing to find a reporter interested in history."

"Uh huh. Well, the paper could stand using some perspective from time to time."

"Yeah, yeah." She paused, flipping through a report on her desk. "I can set you up today—link you to Keppel—but the cost at their end is still quite high, and. . . . You don't mind if I ask you a few questions?"

"No, of course not."

"Could you tell me how the information is going to be used?"

"It's confidential. You know—newspaper work."

"No, you don't understand. I'm not interested in intruding on the privacy of your research. . . . It's, you know, the CIA—Canadian Information Anxiety," she said, looking me in the eye. "If it's going to be published we want a line of credit, something that gets our name out there."

"Sure," I said, rising. "Credit is one thing I can guarantee."

"Then just come with me," she said, and we walked out of her office together.

Near the card catalogues, Ms. Hoffman stopped to type something into a computer. She caught my eye as I watched her pull down icons with the mouse and tap in keyboard codes. "Who would have thought televisions would be in every home. PCs will get there, you watch."

"Call me old fashioned, Ms. Hoffman."

"Call me Vera," she said, smiling.

"Okay . . . Vera."

Vera tapped a bit more, then had me stand before the console. She had small blue earrings, push pins. Round, perfect lobes.

"If you have any questions, I'll be in my office."

"Thanks for your trouble," I said, and in a profusion of apricots she left.

Keppel's library had some stuff on the Iceman. Nervous about starting the personal research, I decided to work up to it, do a test run. I typed in "BRONZE AGE MAN" and "ALPS," where the Iceman was found. It seemed a Mr. Egg examined the body. (Years later, a Mr. Seed would be the scientist to lay claim to the first cloned human child.) Mr. Egg figured the Iceman was either mining or hunting and that he had gotten lost in bad weather. His remains were so intact that forensic scientists were able to tell that a small leather bag he carried contained a repair kit for arrows and that his boots were lined with straw. Carbon dating had yet to be done, but they estimated the remains were four thousand years old. The Iceman had become mummified because the body had thoroughly dried for a year before the climate cooled and snow fell, covering him for the next forty centuries.

I took a deep breath and punched in my parents' names. For my mother and father only one entry appeared. I depressed the enter key and their paid wedding announcement emerged on the screen. Lucas O., my grandfather, and Ida, my grandmother, were mentioned as parents of the groom, but only one man, a Sid from Toronto, brother of my grandfather, my father's uncle, represented the groom's side at the wedding. Furiously, I scribbled down the notes, made a printout. So that was it, I thought. Religion had broken up the family. Nana was a devout Catholic, so much so that she wouldn't even attend her own son's wedding in a Protestant church. Perhaps she'd suffered under Protestants, had some dark personal reasons to hate them. Surely that was part of the story.

Next I tried my father's uncle, the man who came to the wedding. For Sid, only a few lines of an obituary. He'd left an ex-wife and four kids and had worked for years as a motorman in the Toronto subway. My great uncle: a renegade, a bunko artist, maybe. I imagined Nana was disgraced by my father, the Protestant, and Sid, the skip, who not only left his wife and kids, but chose to earn a living ferrying about idle Protestants and Italian Catholics in Toronto's underground. "They deserve each other," she'd have said.

With the printouts spread before me, I tried to visualize what I'd missed, what it must have been like for Nana, a mother growing old alone. How could a mother so totally abandon a son, never see him after his wedding day? I knew people from broken homes, who had fathers that had abandoned them. A reporter friend I knew kept pictures of his mother and brother on his desk, wouldn't even speak of the father who left the family when he was a little boy. But such resentment usually doesn't last a lifetime. At some time resentment gives way to coexistence—late in life, perhaps because of illness or at the birth of a child, someone usually gives in, makes peace, and parent and child get to know each other before the end. How could it be that my father would persist in living a lie that he had no family? The religious break was a part of the problem, I thought, but something else must have happened to cause such a split. Something that had to do with the man about whom nothing had been said, who was not even remembered in a snapshot. I sensed the resentment that drove my father's family apart, kept it apart, had to begin and end with that man, my grandfather.

I breathed deeply, and tapped "LUCAS O.," "CRAWFORD MILL," hit enter and waited. Before long the following words appeared: "Entries before 1940 on microfiche, Keppel Public Library."

I picked up the phone, called the *Star*, and arranged for personal time off. Then I made plans to go north.

As lost souls go, Sir John Franklin was one of a kind. In May 1845, Franklin's two ships, *Erebus* and *Terror*, left an English berth to search for the Northwest Passage. Hip-Hip-Hooray! rang the cheers of the people, the headlines across the country. If anyone could find the northern route to spices and riches in China, Sir Franklin could. Dickens praised him as "the flower of the trained adventurous spirit of the English Navy." The Man Who Survived by Eating His Boots will bring glory to all of England. Hip-Hip-Hooray!

Five of the crew, not up for the trip, were sent home from Greenland, but the remaining one hundred and twenty-nine went on. A whaling vessel near arctic waters saw the ships making good time, sailing toward Baffin Island and Lancaster Sound, the eastern entry to the route to China. Then Sir Franklin and his crew were gone, vanished from the face of the Earth.

Sir Franklin was gallant, but indecisive. If he had lived, a perfect leader for Canada. Tell me what to do and I'll do it. He tried hard but he wasn't up to the task. "With utmost exertion he cannot walk eight miles a day," a fellow traveler said of an earlier journey. Still, he pushed on (or his team of voyageur Canadians and Indians pushed him on) to chart new territory with the hopes of meeting Sir William Parry, his friend and fellow explorer, at Repulse Bay.

They covered thousands of miles. Ten men died. More than one was eaten by the others. Franklin preferred his boots.

If John Franklin were obliged to order the flogging of a malcontent, he'd break out in a cold sweat, throw up. The world is wide enough for both of us, he said of pesky flies. One moment he was there, the innocent of the Arctic: "The White North was thy bones," Tennyson wrote. The next, he was gone. Swallowed whole at the top of the world.

It was early, the Keppel library had yet to open, so I sat down on a bench beside the cenotaph. On November 11th each year, Grandfather, my mother's father, would dress in gray slacks and a red military tunic with two medals attached, and march with hundreds of other old men to the cenotaph in the Armistice parade. Nothing much had changed. Behind me flowed the Sydenham River; cars going to the farmers' market in the former town square filed by. At the end of the parade each year Grandfather held himself ramrod straight, and a calm fell on his face as he observed the minute's silence. Scores of gray-haired men ringed the monument with him in a Stonehenge of flesh and bones that was so still it seemed to evoke the mysterious quiet of the rocks themselves.

My life to that point was about whispers. The sound of the Sydenham, no more than a creek really, a rippling on the surface. Quiet, polite gestures, a tip of the hat. Don't be loud, for goodness' sakes. Here's your plain gray bomber jacket, wool tuque; never a wool-cashmere blend, full-length coat with beret. Know your place. The river does not rush through town on its way to the sea. Waves don't ever crash on shore and erode the streets. Nothing ever changes. Occasionally there's an adjustment, a tweaking, a releasing of air. Anything under such pressure has to give a little before the clamps go down again. When the whispers exhaled, I perked up. It was all there was.

Father, it seemed, had grown up dirt-poor. In a single-parent household for much of his life. There was nothing remarkable in that. A generation before, it was a common enough story, a parent dying when a child needed him most. Typically, it was the mother who died in childbirth; seven to ten children per farm wife was an everyday thing. It was likely that your surviving parent had a similar story; they had lost their own mother or father when they were young, too, or your Uncle Winston or Aunt Bea had, so what was the problem? That was the way things were. It was normal to lose your parents—or at least one of them—along the way. It would be unusual not to. Pray to God if you want to, let Him know your troubles. Get a grip on yourself. Shut your mouth.

But a flood is coming. The Sydenham's banks will overflow like never before. Or an ice age. Every few thousand years, this country is covered in ice. Whatever was once here will be submerged under water or ice, forever hidden from view. What we have here will be gone. Grandfather was wrong, I thought to myself as I sat at the cenotaph that day. The best of Keppel was not underground. The best is in the search, in the uncovering. If we learn nothing, understand nothing, about our lives, about where we come from, then the wedding singer is right. Doing the Hokey Pokey is what it's all about.

From the renovated lobby of the library, Andrew Algee waved at me to come in. I couldn't believe it, after all these years. Pond Scum.

Years ago that was what we called him. Never to his face, of course, true to the boys' creed: adults cannot be trusted so they are never to know. Cruel sarcasm and canny exaggeration, the survivors' natural instincts.

Andrew Algee had been crippled by polio as a boy and always walked with a cane. Old before his time, Algee seemed now as true to his nickname as one could imagine. As if the power of boys had transformed him. His face was badly pock-marked, and one side of his mouth drooped as if it were paralyzed. His long arm strained with the weight of the door and his orangutan hair shook in the breeze as he called me by name to come in.

But adults of learning do not wither under the pressure of the power of boys. They are not evil, calculating, pressing a hidden advantage. Andrew Algee, like many adults of artistic ways in Keppel, had the soul of a medieval Irish monk, methodically inscribing his version of the faith. A few years ago, a psychic had said the same was true of me. I was doing a first-person story on a woman with second sight whom police consulted to solve crimes, whom desperate mothers went to as a last resort to discover the whereabouts of vanished children. She said my aura was all wrong for a journalist. That it was the green of a poet, not the blue of a scribe. You have a very old soul, she said, a religious man, doodling in the margins of an ancient text.

Algee clapped me on the back, said he was glad to see me, that it had been too long. The old man had a perfect memory for sons and daughters of Keppel who had left town to make something of themselves. I was the boy who had done well, gone off to big-city journalism, was working my way to the top.

"Looks better than you can imagine, right, son?" he said, with a sweep of his unsteady hand. We went on a tour of the library, and I had to say I could hardly believe it. Computer terminals lined the north wall near nature studies, and on a split-level second floor the children's department sprawled, with stacks no higher than eye level, a mini-stage, spiffy rockers, fake dinosaurs, and four-color posters of Australian pokorees. Recently, the children's department had won a national design competition and had been submitted as the North American entry in an international challenge. "There's a story for you," Algee said.

"Great, Andrew. Just great . . . but I wonder, could you do me a favor? I'm looking to do some research . . . not anything I can talk about, mind you. For the paper, you know what I mean."

Algee pulled up a tiny wooden chair and plunked himself down. His crippled legs splayed like broken pump handles.

"The Windsor library has given me a start. But I need your library's microfiche for the next stage. I don't need to tell you how important . . ."

Algee struggled to his feet without saying a word and scuttled down the stairs, beckoning me to follow. We went through a passageway to the back of the library and entered a small room in the basement. He directed me to a spanking new microfiche machine and pointed at several file cabinets at the rear of the room that contained the microfiche reels.

"Don't worry. Take all the time you need," Algee said at the door.

"Nobody gets back here without my say-so. You just do what you need to do." Then he closed the heavy door and let me be.

Imagine starving men pulling and pushing a fifteen-hundred-pound weight on a sledge through ice and snow. Every few feet the terrible burden sank and would not budge. With their last remaining strength, twenty men lifted while the rest of Franklin's surviving crew, eighty-five men, pushed and pulled at the sledge until it was freed and on track again. If they went a mile a day, they were lucky. Men dropped dead like stones on a country lane, one after the other, until the last few, unable to push the sledge any farther, curled up under the chief cargo, a boat that was to have taken them into the mouth of Canada. Found with these last survivors of the Franklin expedition, the most tragic to ever have had entered the far north, were such supplies as crested silver plates, monogrammed cutlery, navigation journals, Bibles, novels, bead purses, cigar boxes, and a lightning rod. Among the dead was the corpse of a steward boy, in lightweight clothes, a garment brush and pocket comb at his side.

It was thirteen years after Franklin first set sail that the picture of the final days became clear. Twenty-four men had already died of the cold and starvation when the one hundred and five remaining crew members set off on foot, leaving their damaged, useless ships in the ice-choked channels of the north, and marched to their death.

They did not have to end this way. Eskimos lived on Boothia Peninsula, a ten-day journey east of where their ships were trapped in ice. An experienced explorer, Franklin knew they were there. Others had mapped a course through Simpson Strait, between the mainland and King William Island. Franklin was well aware of this passage, too, but didn't take it. Instead, he turned his ships into an immense twenty- to thirty-foot wall of oncoming ice, an ice pack the size of Norway.

It would be funny if it weren't so tragic. Canada's north was built on a horrible mistake and false pride. The quest for news of Sir John Franklin cost the British government a fortune—675,000 pounds—but gained the north for Canada: Prince of Wales Island, Banks Island, most of Victoria Island, and thousands of square miles of arctic waters and inlets were claimed because of an obsession to find a single wrong-headed man.

We know that Franklin was among the first to die, virtually two years to the day after his ships were last sighted by the northern whalers. But neither his body nor a solitary word written by him on his final voyage has ever been found.

Except for a faded portrait of a young Queen Elizabeth, I was alone in the room. The picture had for years hung above the main circulation desk but now was in the basement. Royalty in Keppel had become like smoking: a habit not easy to admit.

I slipped a microfiche from 1935 onto the machine's reel and began searching. Obituaries ran on the front page, but more often they were inside and were no more than the filler that Cousin John had sent me. I noted down deaths of area namesakes not known to me, proud members of the Knights of Columbus, with brothers in

Guelph, small-town Illinois. There was an infant from Dundalk who died of pneumonia in the winter; another, a teenager, who fell victim to an accidental shooting. But most were farmers with a history of membership in St. Mary's Church, life-long supporters of farm cooperatives.

Later that year a full-page article, first published in the *Toronto Telegram*, detailed the adventures of one District Magistrate J. J., who reminded readers that the north once started in Keppel, Franklin's point of departure. In the area waters, the millkeeper "used to catch sturgeon in nets and keep them in a pool like cattle in a pound, and sell them on the fin to the Indians for ten cents apiece," he wrote. Alvin O., a Toronto resident, was featured the following year in an article about railroad engineers: he was one of three engineers who between them had spent more than one hundred and fifty years on the rails. The article worked best when the reporter just let the men talk, as he did when a fellow engineer, Edwin McConnell, told of being stranded by snow for a week. "A snowplow got through on a Sunday evening and it was like the relief of Ladysmith. Oh, yes, we had been living at the hotel, passengers and all, but the trouble was the farmers couldn't get in and provisions were running low.

"Then we had a corpse with us—a funeral going to Keppel, and there were several mourners. We had to keep the corpse in the freight shed, and the mourners stayed in the hotel. Yes, sir, that was the middle of 1907."

"You don't get things like that now, Ed," Alvin O. remarked.

The newspapers were small then, dailies but usually no more than eight pages. At first it was slow going, because I was reading more than I needed to, the ads to help ease rheumatism pain, the over-written accounts of hockey tilts, but by 1937 I'd hit my stride. Judging from the deaths that made front page—heart attacks of rank Orangemen, the passing of elderly hoteliers, cancers of former presidents of the Bothwell's Corner Red Cross—I began to suspect that the suddenness of my grandfather's death would get front-page play.

Finally, early in 1938, I came upon the story, the top item of the day. The headline was bold, blaring black. At the top there were more headlines than paragraphs, *New York Times* style. I must have read it a hundred times.

AREA FARMER

STEPPED INTO

BOILING TANK

DIED BEFORE MANY WITNESSES

INQUEST TO BE CALLED

An area farmer died on the floor of Crawford's Sawmill Thursday afternoon after being terribly scalded in a pool of boiling water. The Medford Road resident was a frequent visitor to the mill.

Lucas O., 43, had visited the mill during the afternoon to get a load of sawdust and while there had been making a tour of the plant. In leaving, he went out the back and down the jack-ladder used for hauling logs into the mill. He stepped from the ladder into the pool rather than onto the ground. The pool, which is sunk about six feet into the ground, is used for melting ice from frozen logs before they are cut in the mill.

Workers from the mill, attracted by Mr. O's cries for help, hauled him from the tank but he could not be revived. He was declared dead at the scene. An inquest is anticipated.

Mr. O. is survived by his wife, Ida, and two boys. One of the boys, a nine-year-old, had arrived at the mill with his father and was waiting for him in the farm cart.

The schoolhouse crow usually stops at Crawford's Mill around midday. The jet-black bird shrinks in the cold after pecking seeds that surface on the eaves of Medford Road school, then unfolds suddenly on the wing, screeching as he goes. His shadow on the winter floor vanishes long before his laughter does.

Below, my father lunges along the path to the mill, trying to match the adult footprints in the snow. Minutes ago he had finished his sums and been excused by the teacher. With a great effort, my father hadn't glanced back, seen the fear in his brother's eyes, imploring: "Don't go, little brother. Don't you go without me."

The cold stings my father's round, beet-red cheeks but otherwise he's warm. There's no wind in the bush. The brilliant sun darkens scrub trees, stabbing the blue above. It hurts to whistle, to pucker your lips in the cold.

Centuries ago Indians had blazed this path. The biggest of the trees, mostly white pine and red oak, had been notched, and the trail of the few great trees remaining was the most direct way to the mill. Pioneer Keppel exalted the role of purveyor of masts for the British Navy, and the best of the timber on the old Indian trail was harvested for war. Then for premium wallboard, pine chests, and oak dining room sets.

Except for the crunch of his boots on hard-packed snow, my father doesn't make a sound. He had only an apple for lunch, a holdover from the autumn crop, and is hungry and tired. Poor Lyall will be terribly late, he thinks, as he pauses to look back, scans the snowy fields for his brother. He'll get in trouble for being late.

Grandfather is at the farm cart, tightening straps on the harness when Father runs up. "Where's your brother?" he asks. "If he wants a ride home he better not dawdle." Grandfather's lumberjack coat is flecked with wood chips and sawdust; a peak cap pulled to his eyes. My father flinches, averts his gaze. In the light of midday Grandfather is all harsh shadow, angles. He talks as he moves, in short bursts, nothing wasted. When he yanks the axe from under the seat, blinding light from the sun reflects from its blade.

"C'mon, inside then," Lucas says, and the nine-year-old boy follows the man with the axe into the mill. Inside the mill for the first time in his life, Father is stunned by the darkness, left reeling in the entranceway. As his eyes adjust to the unnatural light, he can see the outline of a man who resembles his father, and from the distance of the doorway it looks like the giant, churning blade is bearing down on his father, about to carve him down the middle in one clean cut. Father's cries are not heard in the din, and it is just as well because the change from northern light to an interior lit by dangling naked bulbs, scattered here and there like catacomb torches, distorts perspective in such a way that Grandfather is not close to being killed by a giant blade. Rather, he is in conversation, being thumped on the back by a mill worker who points in Father's direction. Soon Grandfather is stamping his feet and yelling something terrible toward Father, which he can't hear. I mean what kind of a boy, mooning for all the world to see, stands like an idiot at the entrance of a sawmill? What kind of boy makes a fool of his father in that way?

Father runs to Grandfather, who cuffs him hard about the head. What is wrong with you? Listen and learn. When the mill worker hears his offer he begins to chuckle, thumps Grandfather's back again. The axe is only dull, needs a bit of sharpening, but Grandfather jokes about making a trade, a fresh axe for the old one. The man laughs. "Just sharpen it, Luke. Go out the other way, by the pond. Yonder you'll find the grindstone. But mind there's boiling water in the pond. Be careful going out."

His head still throbbing with dull pain, Father doesn't look up but to see the dried horseshit and straw that stick to the soles of his father's boots as he walks two steps behind him. He knows not to drag his feet through the sawdust. Beyond that, he doesn't dare even think.

Father and son go down the jack-ladder, a shortcut to the pond. Not very far down, Grandfather stops because his eyeglasses are fogging up. "Hold the axe," Grandfather grunts to Father, and the boy takes it. Hanging on to the ladder with one hand, my grandfather uses the other to pull off his eyeglasses and begins to wipe them clean. My father, afraid of heights, something he has never dared reveal, begins to grow faint, feels he's about to fall. Slipping, the hand holding the rung comes free as he reaches with the other to stop from falling. "Look out!" he shouts as the axe drops. The blunt end hits Lucas on the forehead as he looks up, startled by the yell. Grandfather descends backward, a black bug upended in moist spray, limbs suspended in air. A loud splash, then sprays of scalding water everywhere. And screams. As if they would never end.

When the mill worker arrives, Father is clinging tightly to the ladder, unable to move. It will take two of them to pry him loose. "Don't worry, little guy, it was an accident. That's how it was. An accident," the mill worker says. Sitting beside my father in the farm cart, the man repeats, "Now, now little guy," over and over again, while Father pulls back on the reins.

green ice

When tons of ice fall from a mountain glacier it's like a meteorite crashing to Earth, leaving a hole millions of times larger than the oversized stone itself. But it's the sound you remember. The rocks below explode on impact. Ice calves, gives birth. It's primal, fearsome, a lion's roar in a megaphone.

In North America more fresh water is locked up in glaciers than in all its lakes and rivers. Billions of tons of ice will fall each day from the face of the tidewater glacier until freeze-up resumes. In the wake of calving bergs, boats have been shipwrecked, dry docks smashed to splinters. Outflow, too, is enormous. During summer melt, an Olympic-sized swimming pool can be filled by a typical northern glacier in less than a minute.

The ice that falls where the land meets the sea is black and blue—black for the rocks torn loose by the force of the ice calving, blue because without bubbles of air, the color of ice is dark, not pale. The size of houses but the weight of skyscrapers, these massifs crash into the sea. It isn't like a house falling; more like if the Brooklyn Bridge were to collapse into the East River.

Icebergs move out to sea. Many look like they can be saddled. They buck, flip over. So many horses in a corral. Others are cabin-size, or broken shards, bergy bits, as far as the eye can see, and the very smallest—growlers—hooded infants, rolling, soon gone, melted away.

At the beach, cars rule. For as long as anyone can remember it's been like that. Big, wide American ones: rebuilt Impalas, Ford Fairlanes, and Buick Skychiefs. But these cars don't gleam, sparkle in blinding light like they do on television. At the beach near my parents' retirement home the sky is never free of clouds, so the light is diffuse and the surface of cars dull, as though they've been badly treated with wax, a bit off, no sheen.

The sand is pressed down by wind and cold and then made even denser by the weight of car wheels. Only the determined children from the bush—from Wiarton, Lion's Head, and The Tub—with hard plastic toys can shape figures from the hard-packed sand. Children from away wear out their soft city-bought utensils quickly, then gather about to watch as the locals construct durable cities and landscapes that stand for weeks.

On days in season a lithe brown girl with long raven hair used to walk gracefully along the sand. She walked with other young girls who had the bodies of their mothers, cross-bred ducks waddling to keep up. The brown girl went into a shack with a sign that said "$5 PER CAR," while the others went on toward The Entrance to shoot pool, bowl a line or two, smoke cigarettes. Motorists would come alongside the shack's opening and without saying a word pay the girl for the right to drive up and down the beach. The sloe-eyed beauty stared straight back at them. But often she was not at the toll booth, and whites laughed as they drove by, flicking glowing cigarette butts into its open door. "Indians," they cried. "What a joke."

Before the building of the Seaway, which dramatically altered shorelines across the Great Lakes, the beach was almost twice as wide from surf to dunes as it is today. In those days young men in crew cuts, their girls in pigtails, cruised their cars up and down the beach, stopping willy-nilly to chat. No one seemed to be going anywhere in particular. Police constables in their padded caps and all-weather tunics called the dispatcher on two-ways, tracing licenses so they could get names and addresses of dishy blondes and brunettes that drove by. Farm pickups and hay wagons, empty after the season, rolled past. Tiny tots at the water's edge would dart occasionally toward the vehicles on the beach. But their parents didn't bite. The rigs weren't moving fast enough. Mostly the cars just sat, like props on a set.

After the Seaway was built, lake levels rose for years until the traffic lanes dwindled to nothing, a winding path of Indian file. Then no cars were allowed, and no one but locals came. For a week in the summer, usually in August, when the water warmed a little, some even swam in the lake.

High water lasted ten years or more. Only recently have the cars come back. Now young men mill about the archway of The Entrance, guzzling beers in Styro sleeves they keep on ice under lock and key in the trunk of the Bel-Air. During the day they work on the line in places like Galt and Kitchener, fitting rubber plugs on metal terminals, sweeping the floor of junk glass, building reputations with air-guns, spinning rivets into place. Most drive hours to get here, to crank up ghetto blasters and scope the horizon for babes. The veterans of hardpack, the local girls, flirt in bikinis two sizes too small with carpenters at the nuclear plant, the best employer in town. Local single men with bellies and arms of spaghetti throw footballs with lifelong chums. Only the painfully thin wear shirts; bald spots glow in the sun. They'll land divorcees of broken dreams, women in conflict and on the rebound, and live for weekend bashes with their buddies and tickets to the Skydome.

Not far from my parents' retirement home, a short-order cook serves the best french fries around. Headbangers with their fat girls in halters flock to the place. For centuries the Indians have been in this place, but only in recent years have they been open for business. The cook dips a soda spoon into a pot and spreads fake gravy over the steaming potatoes. Then ketchup, clear vinegar, a downpour of salt. A gentle bear of a man, he fills one order, then another. Double gravy, extra ketchup. Hold the vinegar.

"Just the fries," I say. Gentle Bear freezes as the dancers do at pow-wows when the drums suddenly stop. Then he looks me in the eye to make sure I'm not kidding. No gravy? The fries are delicious. But locals say they go because it's the cheapest around, because on Indian land there's no GST.

The odd thaw, northern lemmings kill themselves. They run to cliffs with open water below and jump in, frantically trying to swim to the other side. Those in open tundra run themselves to death, perish in convulsions. In forest regions, lemmings drown in rivers, scamper into homes, are killed in traps.

Some scientists say lemmings are prone to a virulent kidney disease. Other experts cite the fragile food source as an explanation. Still others claim that lemmings exhaust their physical resources and die of hypoglycemia. A stranger theory maintains that the mass death comes about from a conflict of personalities: At low population levels a timid but prolific personality is dominant, but at high population levels, an aggressive and less fecund one rules. Eventually this leads to the creature's end.

One autumn there are millions of the wee cuddly creatures, scurrying underfoot, sniffing the air, gobbling grasses. The next spring, none. Perfect individual nests built in the space between the ground and the first layer of snow appear after the thaw. But the lemmings themselves are gone.

My father looks out the picture window from the reupholstered La-Z-Boy at the ice formations on the lake. He designed the house around the view from this room, and in winter he sits for hours and studies the scenery. Gray clouds hug the round, white cliffs that drift across the horizon as far as the eye can see. He's learned to read the weather, so when the ice turns green he stays put. But in the dead of winter, bundled in his Hudson's Bay coat, a fedora jammed on his head, Father goes out alone to the mounds of ice and snow. He likes to stand inside the ice, round, symmetrical, egg-like, and listen. The inside of an unhatched egg. After a deep freeze and brisk winds the walking is easy over the hardpack, and he can go for miles among the snow and ice sculptures. Some are like mountains. Icebergs.

There's a memory about me that Father goes back to. Retired now from selling fireworks, he works when he wants to, doing handyman chores, electrical and plumbing, drywall and sheetrock. He doesn't play cards anymore. In winter he likes to curl. The game on ice, with clean lines and precision, winners and losers. Talk all you want but you have to make the shot. Father will watch curling on television for hours on end, studying, engrossed. Then he snaps off the set and sits, and the memory comes.

A seven-year-old in our neighborhood knew how to handle a stripped willow branch. The largest willow tree around grew in the backyard of Bobby Blair's house, and on Saturdays Bobby selected the best of its branches for his willow whip. Bobby chose a limb of high tensile strength that whistled and snapped. Then he'd slash leaf after leaf from the tree. After he was shooed by his mother from the yard, Bobby went stalking bigger prey.

One Saturday my father was loading bath towels into the trunk in preparation for the trip to the beach when he saw Bobby Blair sneaking around the back of the house, his whip partially hidden behind his back. Helen and I were playing in the sandbox in the side yard. My father had heard our stories of Bobby's cruelty, had seen the red marks on my arms from one previous encounter, so he put down the towels and ran toward us.

But Father was too late. Helen had just moved when Bobby swung his whip or she would have caught the blow in the face. Instead the weapon raked her back, sent her screaming to the door, yelling for my mother. Father would have been upon the boy then, but something in the way I looked stopped him. The bully had hit me twice on the top of the head before I got up and wrenched the whip from his hand, threw it to the ground, and jumped on top of him. My father watched, for longer than he should have, while I straddled Bobby Blair's chest and thrashed him about the face as hard as I could with my fists. Then Father stopped the beating because by watching me he knew that I would not have been able to stop on my own. Violence like this, he told himself, has to be bred in the bone.

Walking in the deliberate hitched stride of a boy more accustomed to broken surfaces than country roads, Lyall drew snickers from Keppel boys when he went into town. Lyall did most of the chores on the family farm. Eight years old when the family moved to take over their homestead near Keppel, Lyall worked with his father in the barn, the orchard, and the fields. For weeks at a time in the fall, Lyall skipped school and joined the hired hands to bring in the apple crop. In winter, he chopped wood in the bush. Spring and summer he worked the fields.

He knew he shouldn't have, but during harvest time, Lyall would conceal two prize apples in his coat and hide them at night in the bedroom he shared with my father in the loft. "After the Fall" apples, the bruised Spys and Macs that were worthless at market, were boy food, my grandfather said. Independent people do not steal from the means of their independence. Do not defy me, boys. Do not eat the market apples.

Night after night, too tired to talk, the boys laid back on their beds, admiring moonbeams, eating their contraband fruit.

In February it was always bitter cold, my father told me. But February of '38 was the worst of them all. The woodstove riser in the loft was the boys' only source of heat, so Lyall and my father slept in the same bed to stay warm. Those nights they'd jump into bed together, burrow under wool blankets, and huddle close.

But one night when they did that, instead of giggling a little and cozying up to my father, Lyall turned away from him toward the wall. He was wheezing and groaning like wind through an overladen tree. Grandfather kept a floodlamp lit near the barn and in that light, as Lyall moved, Father could see he'd gotten two black eyes and a welt on his cheek. He'd complained about Grandfather hitting him, but Father hadn't believed him. Before this, there weren't any red marks or bruises. Lyall was crying, and when he turned to face Father, he showed him his marks.

They heard Grandfather on the stairs. He'd never come up before, it was such a small space, so Father thought he'd just tell them to be quiet, get on to sleep. Soon, stooped but massive in the half-light, Lucas was in the room. Lyall was still and whimpering beside Father. "I want this racket stopped," Grandfather said, swinging his leather belt. In the light of his candle, his angular body and shadow touched the room's every corner. He put the candle down on a rafter. "Do you hear me?" he yelled. "Be quiet!"

Lyall lurched forward beside Father, and Grandfather struck him with such force that the strap broke in the cold. He dropped the shred of strap to the floor and then cursed Lyall for causing him to break the strap, hitting him again and again with his open hand. Father was screaming, telling him to stop, that he'd kill Lyall, but it only seemed to rile him more, to make him hit all the harder, so eventually Father fell quiet. Finally, Grandfather stopped and left.

That was all they'd done: Eaten two apples a night at harvest time. Or all they could figure. Nana tried talking to Grandfather. But there was no use. He had the killer look in his eye. Like mine over the squirming Bobby Blair. To have a terrible temper is like alcoholism—blacking out and denial. One Keppel man escaped to America after a woman he was seeing suddenly disappeared. The story goes that they never found the body and the man never returned or was heard from again. Like death from the cold, death from temper is commonly underreported. In the spring, bodies appear in the East River, the St. Lawrence, the Sydenham, the Thames. Police will tell you unsolved murders most often involve a person whose temper ran amok.

Grandfather put Father to work hand-pumping water to fill the troughs for the cattle. His hands raw and muscles tired and sore, Father would cry like a baby filling that thing, but wouldn't stop until the hundred-gallon trough was filled to the brim. Then Grandfather would have Father spend Saturdays and Sundays in the fields, scrounging for rusty horseshoes, a piece of harness, or hunk of metalwork. Pay him a penny apiece, and then leer at him when he'd find nothing.

"He's gone mad, I guess," folks said, shrugging, looking away. Everyone sure has their problems. After the beating Lyall got in the loft, he didn't go to school for a week. From that day on the boys had to show Grandfather the core of the bruised apples they ate. Lyall showed him the stem.

But Father didn't hate Grandfather the worse for the beatings and abuse. It was for Grandmother that Father hated him. She looked so miserable during this time he thought she'd die. He didn't know if she herself was ever beaten by Grandfather. Up until Grandfather's death, Father was sure of one thing: If that man had touched his mother, he would have killed him. The horror for Father would have been not killing him.

The packing is never good on the coldest of days. It's not a matter of strength—the snow will fly apart, blow away in the wind. The snow was like this the day my father went to meet Grandfather at the mill.

His breath hovering around him in the still air, my father stumbled and lurched in the loose snow. He'd stayed later than expected at school to finish an assignment, a drawing of a barn and farmhouse, and was moving quickly to the mill to meet his father in the parking lot as they'd planned. If he were late, my father thought, he'd be cracked about the back with a new leather thong. On the road home aboard the farm cart, traveling down a cold and snowy path with low-hanging branches, Lucas O. would thrash him because he had been late.

The horse and farm cart were there when he arrived. Exhausted and gasping for air, my father ran up to the cart and leaned against it. The sweat cooling under his wool long johns made him feverish, trembling. Sled dogs without tails will die in the cold, choke on the freezing air. Finally, he pushed off the cart and hugged the horse around the neck for warmth. Then, drying the last of his tears, he walked on slowly to the mill.

The windows were caked thick with frost, but not the one by the exit door, which was dabbed with moisture, so it caught my father's eye. He pulled himself up to look through the window and saw a man who looked like his father lying on the floor of the mill, dripping wet. Workers were running every which way. One with a pair of scissors was cutting Lucas's clothes into shreds.

The contorted face of his father looked up and for an instant their eyes met. "Go home," my father read on the lips of the man pointing toward the door. "Go home." Then men, frantic and unthinking, stood in his way and waved at the boy to shoo.

My father rode the horse and cart home as fast as he could. Nana was blacking the woodstove. He told her what he'd seen, and she dropped the rag to her side and grabbed my father by the shoulders. "Take me," she said. "Take me to the hospital." Nana cried softly, huddled beside my father. A doctor said Lucas had died on the floor of the mill. The last words he'd managed were directed at my father, the boy at the window.

Grandfather died on that day, February 16. And no one will ever know the real truth about it. They say he went into the mill alone; a coroner's inquest ruled that he died accidentally, that his glasses fogged over and he became disoriented and slipped from the jack-ladder above a pit of boiling water and fell to his death.

That was how the authorities saw it. But people talked. During winter in the Keppel sawmill only Grandfather used the jack-ladder, a risky shortcut over a boiling vat of water used to de-ice timber. Perhaps the ladder had been tampered with. Keppel police never thoroughly investigated. Grandfather's violence was extreme but mostly confined to the family. Still, there was one incident. Once in the days before his death, Grandfather lost his temper with a friend of Nana's, a woman who had come over for tea to flip through some canvases. Not the wild, dark ones, the open wounds she'd taken to working on during this period, but the earlier ones, the landscapes and snow watchers, the ones that might sell.

He'd never lost it with people before, Nana found herself saying. She and her children had ceased to exist. As anyone who has endured abuse will tell you, the worst is what you can't see.

Who else had motive but the children, the wife, a woman entrapped by a man with a disease? Would Grandmother have done such a thing? If not, then who? Perhaps it was just as they say, an accident. God's way of evening the score. In a year or two after

Grandfather's death, Lyall was fourteen and out of the house to earn a living, never to return. A widow with a ten-year-old son in the Depression, Grandmother sold corsets door to door, earned a pittance from the landscapes of mud season she would never stop making. After the war, she started the first welfare office for the rural poor, wretched broken people she filled out forms for. She'd come to their doors in the night, and in her presence the fighting and drinking stopped—if only for a while.

Nana would die respected in Keppel, the painter woman, a mother of broken dreams. But in the end it was only strangers she could reach out to. The final years it wasn't just Father she didn't see. Nana refused to leave the house, spurned anyone who told her to sell, leave the past behind. Telephone linemen knew nothing of her because phones were never installed. Even electric meter readers did their work from a pole on the county road because she did not want them coming around. Perhaps she lived with a secret. Who can say? She suffered, my father said. Like us all.

Travel to the far north is common now. You can go through the Northwest Passage, direct to the place where the Franklin party went down. Finger the fragments once held by the doomed adventurers.

In recent years, I've been traveling more often back to Sauble Beach to visit my parents. I like winter best. Twisted spare bushes clot the dunes against the nickel-colored sky. The bushes are cut by wind and cold so that only hard, bony shapes remain. Except for the occasional bounding mutt there are no signs of life.

Once, a blizzard hit. Father has a new snowblower, and when

snow starts to collect he drags his snowsuit into the living room and puts it on. Above the mantle is a framed photograph by Ned Pendleton, whose photos of daily life in Keppel were often displayed in the town art gallery. The picture was taken at the peak of Father's career in fireworks display: Father piling mortars into the back of a panel wagon. He touches the blue pebble he had saved for Mum a lifetime ago, pulls down the balaclava over his face so that only his coal eyes emerge, and goes looking for his boots.

In no time at all several feet of snow have fallen, and Father is outside in the back clearing a path. I'm going out for a walk and move toward him. He stops what he's doing and for a moment we both pause. I realize that I have never before seen Father in a snowsuit, the clothes of a northern child. Not an eyelash is visible. I, too, am a little boy again, thinking that Father is something else, an alien, a storm trooper. Suddenly, in a violent shooing motion, he waves at me to go on. Get out of the way. There is a gust of wind, and snow engulfs us both. When the blowing snow lifts, Father returns to his task, pushing snow in another direction, moving on down the lane.

acknowledgments

I would like to extend my thanks to many people without whom this book would never have come to be. I would like to thank my wife, Mary Morris, who read an opening sequence about a young boy watching his father flood a rink, and suggested a memoir, and even a title. I would also like to thank Christopher Merrill, who read parts of the book a decade ago and then directed me at the right time to the right person, Barbara Ras, my editor, whose support has been invaluable to me. I also want to thank agent Diana Finch for her support and enthusiasm, and Lizzie Grossman, whose optimism encouraged me. Many hours were spent on northern research and reading tales of arctic lore, and I feel I must give special mention to the writings of Farley Mowat, *Arctic Dreams* by Barry Lopez, *The*

Arctic Grail by Pierre Berton, *The Discovery of Slowness* by Sten Nadolny, *Roughing It in the Bush* by Susannah Moodie, and *American Dreamers* by Clarice Stasz, which were particularly helpful to me. I also want to thank Siri Hustvedt and John Blanton for their careful readings and encouragement and for the support of Rena Shulsky and Brian Ashley. And finally I want to thank my parents, Bill and Barbara O'Connor, who have never strayed in their belief and trust in me and my writing.

1889